HEALTH CARE ISSUES, COSTS AND ACCESS

DISPROPORTIONATE MEDICAID EXPENDITURES

SELECT ANALYSES

HEALTH CARE ISSUES, COSTS AND ACCESS

Additional books in this series can be found on Nova's website under the Series tab.

Additional e-books in this series can be found on Nova's website under the e-book tab.

HEALTH CARE ISSUES, COSTS AND ACCESS

DISPROPORTIONATE MEDICAID EXPENDITURES

SELECT ANALYSES

CASSIE PAVESI
EDITOR

New York

LIBRARY OF CONGRESS CATALOGING-IN-PUBLICATION DATA

ISBN: 978-1-63321-118-6

Published by Nova Science Publishers, Inc. † New York

CONTENTS

PREFACE

This book examines high-expenditure Medicaid-only beneficiaries, considering states' spending on them compared with all other Medicaid beneficiaries; their key characteristics; and their service usage compared with all other Medicaid-only beneficiaries. This book also provides an overview of Medicaid disproportionate share hospital DSH). It includes a description of the rules delineating how state DSH allotments are calculated and the exceptions to the rules, how DSH hospitals are defined, and how DSH payments are calculated.

Chapter 1 – Medicaid is an important source of health coverage for millions of low- income individuals. Research on Medicaid has demonstrated that a small percentage of beneficiaries account for a disproportionately large share of Medicaid expenditures. Understanding states' expenditures for high-expenditure populations—both those dually eligible for Medicare and Medicaid, and those who are Medicaid- only—could enhance efforts to manage Medicaid expenditures.

GAO was asked to examine the demographics and service usage of Medicaid beneficiaries, particularly those who are not eligible for Medicare. This report examines high- expenditure Medicaid-only beneficiaries, considering (1) states' spending on them compared with all other Medicaid beneficiaries; (2) their key characteristics; and (3) their service usage compared with all other Medicaid-only beneficiaries.

GAO analyzed beneficiary and expenditure data from the Medicaid Statistical Information System Annual Person Summary File for 2009, the most recent year available at the time GAO conducted its work. GAO defined high-expenditure beneficiaries as those with total expenditures in the top 5 percent of expenditures within each state. GAO combined these data at a national level, and analyzed the characteristics associated with being a high-expenditure beneficiary, the probability of being a high-expenditure Medicaid beneficiary, and what services contributed to high expenditures.

Chapter 2 – The Medicaid statute requires states to make disproportionate share hospital (DSH) payments to hospitals treating large numbers of low-income patients. This provision is intended to recognize the disadvantaged financial situation of those hospitals because low-income patients are more likely to be uninsured or Medicaid enrollees. Hospitals often do not receive payment for services rendered to uninsured patients, and Medicaid provider payment rates are generally lower than the rates paid by Medicare and private insurance.

As with most Medicaid expenditures, the federal government reimburses states for a portion of their Medicaid DSH expenditures based on each state's federal medical assistance percentage (FMAP). While most federal Medicaid funding is provided on an open-ended basis, federal Medicaid DSH funding is capped. Each state receives an annual DSH allotment, which is the maximum amount of federal matching funds that each state is permitted to claim for Medicaid DSH payments. In FY2012, federal DSH allotments totaled $11.4 billion.

The health insurance coverage provisions of the Patient Protection and Affordable Care Act (ACA, P.L. 111-148 as amended) are expected to reduce the number of uninsured individuals in the United States, which means there should be less need for Medicaid DSH payments. As a result, the ACA included a provision directing the Secretary of the Department of Health and Human Services to make aggregate reductions in federal Medicaid DSH allotments for each year from FY2014 to FY2020. Since the ACA, three laws have amended the DSH reductions. The Supreme Court's decision regarding the ACA Medicaid expansion does not impact these DSH reduction amounts, but states' decisions about implementing the ACA Medicaid expansion could impact the allocation of the DSH reductions across states starting in FY2016.

While there are some federal requirements that states must follow in defining DSH hospitals and calculating DSH payments, for the most part, states are provided significant flexibility. One way the federal government restricts states' Medicaid DSH payments is that the federal statute limits the amount of DSH payments for Institutions for Mental Disease and other mental health facilities.

Since Medicaid DSH allotments were implemented in FY1993, total Medicaid DSH expenditures (i.e., including federal and state expenditures) have remained relatively stable. Over this same period of time, total Medicaid

DSH expenditures as a percentage of total Medicaid medical assistance expenditures (i.e., including both federal and state expenditures but excluding expenditures for administrative activities) dropped from 13% to 4%.

This report provides an overview of Medicaid DSH. It includes a description of the rules delineating how state DSH allotments are calculated and the exceptions to the rules, how DSH hospitals are defined, and how DSH payments are calculated. The DSH allotment section includes information about how the ACA DSH reductions may be allocated among the states, and the possible implications of the Supreme Court's decision regarding the ACA Medicaid expansion. The DSH expenditures section shows the trends in DSH spending and explains variation in states' DSH expenditures. Finally, the basic requirements for state DSH reports and independently certified audits are also outlined.

In: Disproportionate Medicaid Expenditures ISBN: 978-1-63321-118-6
Editor: Cassie Pavesi

Chapter 1

MEDICAID: DEMOGRAPHICS AND SERVICE USAGE OF CERTAIN HIGH-EXPENDITURE BENEFICIARIES*

United States Government Accountability Office

WHY GAO DID THIS STUDY

Medicaid is an important source of health coverage for millions of low-income individuals. Research on Medicaid has demonstrated that a small percentage of beneficiaries account for a disproportionately large share of Medicaid expenditures. Understanding states' expenditures for high-expenditure populations—both those dually eligible for Medicare and Medicaid, and those who are Medicaid- only—could enhance efforts to manage Medicaid expenditures.

GAO was asked to examine the demographics and service usage of Medicaid beneficiaries, particularly those who are not eligible for Medicare. This report examines high- expenditure Medicaid-only beneficiaries, considering (1) states' spending on them compared with all other Medicaid beneficiaries; (2) their key characteristics; and (3) their service usage compared with all other Medicaid-only beneficiaries.

* This is an edited, reformatted and augmented version of the United States Government Accountability Office publication, GAO-14-176, dated February 2014.

GAO analyzed beneficiary and expenditure data from the Medicaid Statistical Information System Annual Person Summary File for 2009, the most recent year available at the time GAO conducted its work. GAO defined high-expenditure beneficiaries as those with total expenditures in the top 5 percent of expenditures within each state. GAO combined these data at a national level, and analyzed the characteristics associated with being a high-expenditure beneficiary, the probability of being a high-expenditure Medicaid beneficiary, and what services contributed to high expenditures.

WHAT GAO FOUND

In fiscal year 2009, states spent nearly a third (31.6 percent) of all Medicaid expenditures on the most expensive Medicaid-only beneficiaries, who were 4.3 percent of total Medicaid beneficiaries. States spent another third (33.1 percent) on all other Medicaid-only beneficiaries, who represented 81.2 percent of total Medicaid beneficiaries. Among dual eligible beneficiaries, a similar pattern existed, with a small proportion of the population accounting for a disproportionate share of expenditures.

Certain characteristics significantly increased the probability of being a high- expenditure Medicaid-only beneficiary. Specifically, the results of GAO's analyses indicate that the probability of being a high-expenditure Medicaid-only beneficiary was:

- 24.4 percent for those residing in a long-term care facility,
- 20.8 percent for those with human immunodeficiency virus/acquired immunodeficiency syndrome,
- 18.3 percent for those with disabilities, and
- 13.3 percent for new mothers or infants.

Overall, hospital services and long-term services and supports in non-institutional and institutional settings comprised nearly 65 percent of the total expenditures for high-expenditure Medicaid-only beneficiaries, with smaller proportions for drugs, payments to managed care organizations and premium assistance, and non- hospital acute care. In contrast to high-expenditure beneficiaries, payments to managed care organizations and premium assistance comprised 57.2 percent of total expenditures for all other Medicaid-only beneficiaries.

HHS provided technical comments on a draft of this report, which were incorporated as appropriate.

ABBREVIATIONS

CHIP	Children's Health Insurance Program
CMS	Centers for Medicare & Medicaid Services
FPL	federal poverty level
HHS	Department of Health and Human Services
HIV/AIDS	human immunodeficiency virus/acquired immunodeficiency syndrome
HMO	health maintenance organization
LTC	long-term care
LTSS	long-term services and supports
MSIS	Medicaid Statistical Information System
PPACA	Patient Protection and Affordable Care Act

February 19, 2014

The Honorable Charles E. Grassley
United States Senate

Dear Senator Grassley:

Medicaid, a joint federal-state program for certain low-income individuals, is an important source of health coverage for millions of children, adults, aged individuals (individuals aged 65 and older), and those with disabilities. In fiscal year 2012, the Medicaid program spent approximately $435.5 billion to provide health care services to about 72.6 million beneficiaries. Additionally, Medicaid enrollment is likely to grow within states that choose to expand eligibility for Medicaid in response to the Patient Protection and Affordable Care Act of 2010 (PPACA).[1] The Congressional Budget Office estimated that, as a result of PPACA, 10 million additional people could be enrolled in Medicaid and the Children's Health Insurance Program (CHIP) by 2016 compared with 2012.[2] Within Medicaid, there are two groups of beneficiaries—one composed of individuals who are only enrolled in Medicaid, and another composed of individuals enrolled in both Medicaid and Medicare, commonly referred to as dual-eligible beneficiaries.[3]

Research on Medicaid enrollment and spending has demonstrated that a small percentage of beneficiaries account for a disproportionately large share of Medicaid expenditures. Understanding states' expenditures for both high-expenditure populations—those dually eligible and those who are Medicaid-only—could enhance efforts to manage Medicaid expenditures for particular types of beneficiaries.

You asked us to provide information on the demographics and service usage of different types of high-expenditure Medicaid beneficiaries, noting that less attention has been paid to the demographics and service utilization of high-expenditure Medicaid-only beneficiaries compared with dual-eligible beneficiaries. In this report, we examine (1) states' spending for high-expenditure beneficiaries, both Medicaid-only and dual-eligible beneficiaries, compared with other Medicaid beneficiaries; (2) the characteristics associated with high-expenditure Medicaid-only beneficiaries; and (3) the services that contributed to high expenditures for Medicaid-only beneficiaries, and how they compared with service usage by all other Medicaid-only beneficiaries.

To examine states' spending for high-expenditure Medicaid-only beneficiaries compared with other Medicaid beneficiaries, we used data from the fiscal year 2009 Medicaid Statistical Information System (MSIS) Annual Person Summary File.[4] We first calculated the total number of Medicaid enrollees and total Medicaid expenditures in each state separately for both the Medicaid-only and dual-eligible beneficiaries.[5] We then determined the number of beneficiaries whose total expenditures fell within the top 5 percent of total expenditures within each state for each of these groups, designating them as high-expenditure beneficiaries. Finally, we calculated the total expenditures for high-expenditure Medicaid-only beneficiaries and all other Medicaid-only beneficiaries in each state, and combined these data at a national level.

To examine the characteristics associated with high-expenditure Medicaid-only beneficiaries, we determined the percentage of high-expenditure Medicaid-only beneficiaries with key characteristics and used logistic regression to examine the effect of having key beneficiary characteristics on the probability of being a high-expenditure Medicaid- only beneficiary.[6] The key beneficiary characteristics represented as independent variables in our logistic regression model included: eligibility group (disabled, child, adult, aged), age, gender, race/ethnicity, geographic location,[7] participation in capitated managed care,[8] period of enrollment in Medicaid (whether full year or partial year), as well as whether the beneficiaries had any of five health conditions or had received any of two services.[9] Finally, our logistic regression models included characteristics of states' Medicaid programs, such as their spending on high-expenditure beneficiaries and long-term services and supports (LTSS) in non-institutional settings (also called home and community based services) and capitated managed care penetration rates.[10] We report percentages that describe the high-expenditure beneficiary population, as well as the probabilities that demonstrate the association of each characteristic with the likelihood of being in the high- expenditure group.

To examine the services that contributed to high expenditures for Medicaid-only beneficiaries and how they compared with service usage by all other Medicaid-only beneficiaries, we determined the distribution of expenditures for high-expenditure Medicaid-only beneficiaries. The data allowed us to describe patterns of usage for the following six service categories: (1) hospital care, (2) non-hospital acute care, (3) drugs, (4) managed care and premium assistance,[11] (5) LTSS in non-institutional settings, and (6) LTSS in institutional settings.[12] We compared their distribution to those of all other Medicaid-only beneficiaries.

We assessed the reliability of the 2009 MSIS Annual Summary File data we received from the Centers for Medicare & Medicaid Services (CMS) by performing appropriate electronic data checks and by interviewing agency officials who were knowledgeable about the data. This allowed us to determine that the data were suitable for our purposes. We retained approximately 64.5 million of the original 71.6 million records (90 percent) for our analysis; the majority of exclusions were due to unknown eligibility status. For a more complete description of our methodology, see appendix I.

We conducted this performance audit from September 2012 through February 2014 in accordance with generally accepted government auditing standards. Those standards require that we plan and perform our work to obtain sufficient, appropriate evidence to provide a reasonable basis for our findings and conclusions based on our audit objectives. We believe that the evidence obtained provides a reasonable basis for our findings and conclusions based on our audit objectives.

Background

At the federal level, CMS, within the Department of Health and Human Services (HHS), is responsible for overseeing the design and operation of states' Medicaid programs, and states administer their respective Medicaid programs' day-to-day operations.

In conformance with federal requirements, states establish beneficiaries' eligibility for Medicaid, and determine the services that will be provided to beneficiaries and how they will be provided in their state.

Medicaid Eligibility and Financing

Eligibility for Medicaid is based on a variety of categorical and financial requirements. Historically, categories of Medicaid eligibility included pregnant women, low-income children and their parents, individuals who are aged, and individuals with disabilities. In 2014, certain low-income adults who did not fall into one of these groups may be eligible for Medicaid in states that chose to expand coverage to these individuals under PPACA. Dual-eligible beneficiaries, who are eligible for both Medicaid and Medicare, generally fall into two categories: (1) low-income seniors (individuals aged 65 years old and over) and (2) individuals with disabilities under the age of 65.

While some characteristics of state programs vary, Medicaid generally covers a wide range of health care services. These include hospital care; outpatient services, such as physician services, laboratory and other diagnostic tests; prescription drugs; dental care; and LTSS in institutions and in the community.[13] Non-institutional LTSS include home health and personal care services, among other services. Medicaid is the nation's primary payer for LTSS, and provided approximately 41 percent of LTSS funding in the United States in 2010.[14]

As we have previously reported, nearly all states enroll some Medicaid beneficiaries in a form of managed care.[15] States vary widely in terms of the scope of services they provide and the populations they enroll in managed care. Some states contract with managed care organizations to provide the full range of covered Medicaid services to certain enrollees, for which they pay a set, or capitated, amount per member per month. Alternatively, states may rely on arrangements, such as limited benefit plans—which provide a limited set of services, including dental care or behavioral health services—or primary care case management programs in which enrollees are assigned a primary care provider who is responsible for providing primary care services and for coordinating other needed health care. States often provide long-term care services outside of managed care arrangements.[16]

Service Utilization and Expenditures among Medicaid Beneficiaries

Researchers have examined patterns of service utilization and expenditures within the Medicaid population, with a number of articles focused on dual-eligible beneficiaries. For example, one study examining Medicaid enrollment and expenditures found that dual-eligible beneficiaries comprised 14 percent of all Medicaid enrollees, but 36 percent of Medicaid expenditures in 2010.[17] Studies focused on dual-eligible beneficiaries have further found that a small proportion of these beneficiaries were responsible for a significant portion of Medicaid expenditures spent on dual-eligible beneficiaries. For example, one study found that in 2007 full benefit dual-eligible beneficiaries who were in the top 10 percent of Medicaid spending were responsible for 51 percent of Medicaid spending on dual-eligible beneficiaries.[18]

The research also indicates that there is a subset of Medicaid-only beneficiaries who are very costly, such as those with institutional care needs or chronic conditions. One study showed that high-expenditure Medicaid beneficiaries in 2001 included subgroups from each eligibility category, with the elderly and disabled making up the greatest shares of this high-expenditure group. The largest portions of spending were for hospital care for children and adults, intermediate care for individuals with disabilities, and nursing home care for the elderly.[19]

Another study showed that annual per capita expenditures ranged from $8,000 to nearly $16,000 for Medicaid beneficiaries with chronic conditions, including asthma, coronary heart disease, congestive heart failure, diabetes, or hypertension. This study also noted that annual per capita expenditures may double and sometimes triple when single chronic conditions are coupled with mental illness and a drug or alcohol disorder.[20]

Nearly One-Third of States' Medicaid Expenditures Were for High-Expenditure Medicaid-Only Beneficiaries

High-expenditure Medicaid-only beneficiaries accounted for almost a third of states' total Medicaid expenditures. When aggregated at the national level, states spent 31.6 percent of Medicaid expenditures on these beneficiaries, who represented 4.3 percent of all beneficiaries. States spent another 33.1 percent of Medicaid expenditures on all other Medicaid-only beneficiaries, who represented 81.2 percent of total Medicaid beneficiaries. The last 35.2 percent of state Medicaid expenditures went for dual-eligible Medicaid beneficiaries. States spent 13.3 percent of total Medicaid expenditures on high-cost dual-eligible beneficiaries (less than 1 percent of the total Medicaid population) and 21.9 percent of total Medicaid expenditures on other dual-eligible beneficiaries (13.8 percent of total Medicaid beneficiaries). (See figure 1).

At the beneficiary level, per-capita spending on high-expenditure Medicaid-only beneficiaries greatly exceeded that of all other Medicaid- only beneficiaries, but was less than what was spent on high-expenditure dual-eligible beneficiaries. (See table 1.) Overall, per capita spending by states on high-expenditure Medicaid-only beneficiaries was approximately 18 times higher than per capita spending on all other Medicaid-only beneficiaries. This was similar to the pattern of spending for dual-eligible beneficiaries, with per capita spending significantly higher for high- expenditure dual-eligible beneficiaries compared with all other dual- eligible beneficiaries.

Table 1. Per Capita Spending by Beneficiary Group, Fiscal Year 2009

Beneficiary group	Per capita spending, high-expenditure beneficiaries	Per capita spending, all other beneficiaries
Medicaid-only	\$35,983	\$1,989
Dual-eligible	\$89,440	\$7,762

Source: GAO analysis of Centers for Medicare & Medicaid Services' data.

Note: Medicaid-only beneficiaries are eligible for Medicaid but not Medicare. Dual-eligible beneficiaries are eligible for Medicare and Medicaid. Medicaid-only and dual–eligible beneficiaries may also have other sources of health care coverage. High-expenditure beneficiaries represent those whose total expenditures fell within the top 5 percent of total expenditures within each state.

At the state level, there was wide variation in spending per capita on high-expenditure Medicaid-only beneficiaries. (See figure 2.) Per-capita expenditures by state per beneficiary ranged from \$20,896 to \$83,365.[21]

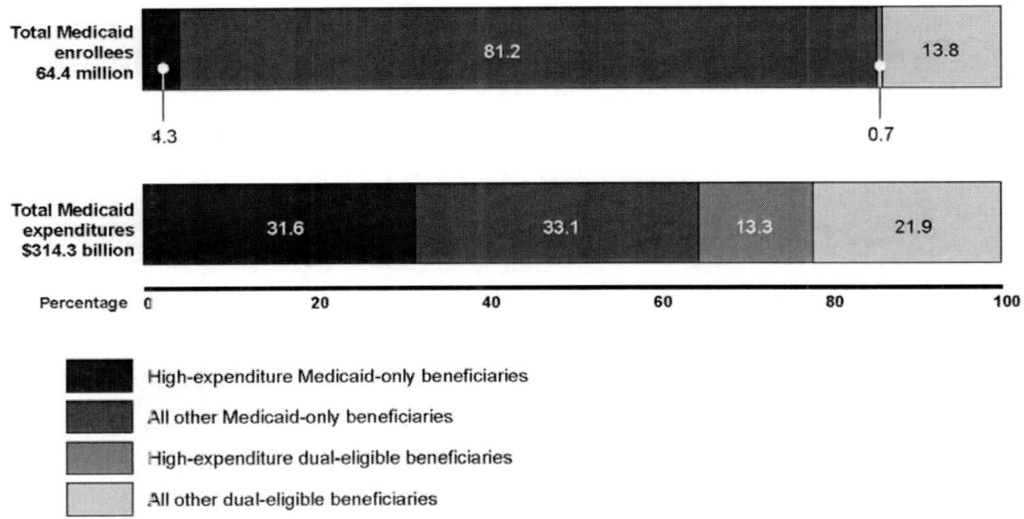

Source: GAO analysis of Centers for Medicare & Medicaid Services data.

Note: Dual-eligible beneficiaries are eligible for Medicare and Medicaid. Medicaid-only beneficiaries are eligible for Medicaid but not Medicare.

Both dual-eligible and Medicaid-only beneficiaries may also have other sources of health care coverage. High-expenditure beneficiaries represent those whose total expenditures fell within the top 5 percent of total expenditures within each state for their group—Medicaid-only or dual-eligible beneficiaries. All other beneficiaries represent those whose spending for their group was less than the spending for the top 5 percent. Percentages may not add to 100 due to rounding.

Figure 1. Percent of Total Medicaid Expenditures by Beneficiary Spending Group, Fiscal Year 2009.

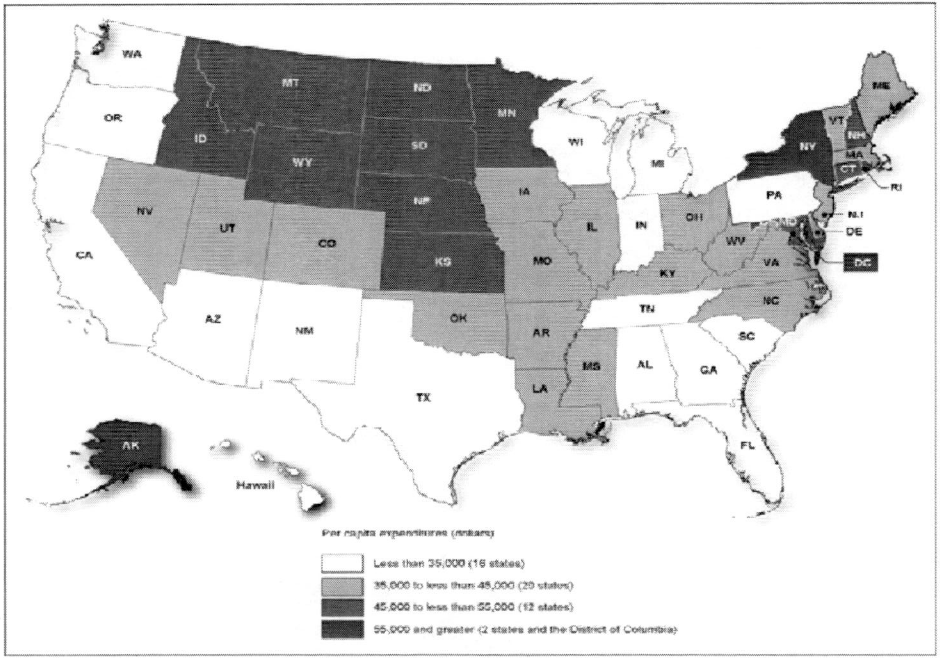

Source: GAO analysis of Centers for Medicare & Medicaid Services data; Map Resources (map).

Note: Medicaid-only beneficiaries are eligible for Medicaid but not Medicare. Medicaid-only beneficiaries may also have other sources of health care coverage. High-expenditure beneficiaries represent those whose total expenditures fell within the top 5 percent of total expenditures within each state.

Figures include beneficiaries with restricted benefits, such as those who only receive family planning benefits.

Figure 2. State Variation in Per Capita Spending on High-Expenditure Medicaid-Only Beneficiaries, Fiscal Year 2009.

Disability, Certain Conditions, Delivery/ Childbirth, and Long-Term Care Residency Were Strongly Associated with Being a High-Expenditure Medicaid-Only Beneficiary

Key characteristics—such as having a disability, having certain conditions, delivery/childbirth, and residing in a LTC facility—were strongly associated with being a high-expenditure Medicaid-only beneficiary. These key characteristics had consistently strong associations with being a high-expenditure Medicaid-only beneficiary even when the data were examined separately for each eligibility group.[22]

Table 2. Percentage and Estimated Probability of Being a High-Expenditure Medicaid-Only Beneficiary by Eligibility Group, Fiscal Year 2009

Eligibility Category	Percentage of high-expenditure population	Probability of being a high- expenditure beneficiary (percent)
Child	16.1	2.0
Adult	15.0	2.6
Aged	2.5	10.5
Disabled	66.3	18.3

Source: GAO analysis of Centers for Medicare & Medicaid Services' data.

Note: High-expenditure beneficiaries represent those whose total expenditures fell within the top 5 percent of total expenditures within each state. All other beneficiaries represent those whose spending was less than the spending for the top 5 percent. Medicaid-only beneficiaries are eligible for Medicaid but not Medicare.

Probabilities were derived from logistic regression results. A probability greater than 5 percent indicates that a characteristic's influence on the beneficiary being in the high-expenditure group was more than what would have occurred by chance alone. All probabilities were significant at the 0.05 level.

We found that about two-thirds of the high-expenditure group was comprised of beneficiaries who were eligible for Medicaid due to disability.[23] Further, the probability of being a high-expenditure Medicaid- only beneficiary was 18.3 percent for disabled Medicaid-only beneficiaries, which was higher than for any other eligibility group. (See table 2.)

In contrast, non-disabled children and adult beneficiaries each had less than a 3 percent probability of being in the high-expenditure group, but made up 16.1 and 15 percent, respectively, of the high- expenditure Medicaid-only beneficiaries.

Residing in a long-term care (LTC) facility or having certain conditions, such as human immunodeficiency virus/acquired immunodeficiency syndrome (HIV/AIDS), was also strongly associated with being a high- expenditure Medicaid-only beneficiary. (See table 3.) We found that while beneficiaries residing in a LTC facility comprised 8.8 percent of the Medicaid-only high-expenditure group, they had a 24.2 percent probability of being high-expenditure beneficiaries. Regarding the impact of certain conditions, beneficiaries with HIV/AIDS comprised just 3.4 percent of the high-expenditure group, but had a 20.8 percent probability of being high-expenditure beneficiaries.

Additionally, delivery/childbirth—giving birth for the mother or being born for the infant—increased the probability of being a high-cost beneficiary. New mothers and infants were 9.8 percent of the high-expenditure population, but had a 13.3 percent probability of being high-expenditure beneficiaries. (See app. II for characteristics of high- expenditure beneficiaries.)

We also found that while demographic factors like age and race, capitated managed care participation, and characteristics of the state where the beneficiary was enrolled helped to describe the Medicaid-only population,[24] these factors were generally less strongly associated with being a high-expenditure beneficiary. (See app. III for a complete table of probabilities.)

In addition, we used logistic regression to examine the factors that influence the probability of being a high-expenditure beneficiary separately for each of the four eligibility groups (children, adults, aged, and disabled). We found that having one of the identified conditions or using one of the included services was consistently associated with a greater probability of being a high-expenditure Medicaid-only beneficiary compared with those without such characteristics.

However, the size of their influence differed. For example, children had an 11.4 percent probability of being high-expenditure Medicaid-only beneficiaries if they had HIV/AIDS, but individuals with disabilities had a 71.6 percent probability if they had that condition. (See app. III for complete table of probabilities.)

Table 3. Percentage and Estimated Probability of Being a High-Expenditure Medicaid-Only Beneficiary, by Selected Conditions and Services, Fiscal Year 2009

Characteristic	Percentage Of high -expenditure population	Probability of being a high-expenditure beneficiary (percent)
Conditions		
HIV/AIDS[a]	3.4	20.8
Mental health condition	51.8	9.1
Diabetes	18.6	8.8
Substance abuse	19.1	7.9
Asthma	14.5	6.8
Services		
Long-term care residence	8.8	24.2
Delivery/childbirth[b]	9.8	13.3

Source: GAO analysis of Centers for Medicare & Medicaid Services' data.

Note: High-expenditure beneficiaries represent those whose total expenditures fell within the top 5 percent of total expenditures within each state. All other beneficiaries represent those whose spending was less than the spending for the top 5 percent. Medicaid-only beneficiaries are eligible for Medicaid but not Medicare.

Probabilities were derived from logistic regression results. A probability greater than 5 percent indicates that a characteristic's influence on the beneficiary being in the high-expenditure group was more than what would have occurred by chance alone. All probabilities were significant at the 0.05 level.

[a] HIV/AIDS stands for human immunodeficiency virus/acquired immunodeficiency syndrome.

[b] Delivery/childbirth may include costs attributed to a mother during delivery or the child soon after birth.

High-Expenditure Beneficiaries Had High Hospital Expenditures and Significantly Different Spending Patterns Compared with All Other Medicaid-Only Beneficiaries

Overall, hospital services and LTSS represented the bulk of spending for high expenditure Medicaid-only beneficiaries—almost 65 percent. In contrast, payments to managed care organizations and premium assistance constituted the largest proportion of expenditures for all other Medicaid-only beneficiaries. In addition, when we examined Medicaid- only high-expenditure and other beneficiaries separately by eligibility group, the differences in service use were generally consistent, but the proportion of expenditures for the different services varied. Separately examining high-expenditure Medicaid-only beneficiaries in LTC institutions and beneficiaries with spending in the top 1 percent of expenditures showed that these beneficiaries had the highest spending for hospital services and LTSS.

Spending Patterns for All High-Expenditure Medicaid-Only Beneficiaries Compared with All Other Medicaid- Only Beneficiaries

For high-expenditure Medicaid-only beneficiaries as a whole, hospital services comprised 30.6 percent, LTSS in non-institutional settings comprised 24.3 percent, and LTSS in institutions comprised 9.7 percent of their expenditures. Other expenditures were for drugs, managed care and premium assistance, and non-hospital acute care. In contrast to high-expenditure Medicaid-only beneficiaries, the largest share of total expenditures for all other Medicaid-only beneficiaries was for managed care and premium assistance (57.2 percent), followed by non-hospital acute care (16.6 percent), hospital services (11.9 percent), drugs (9.7 percent) and LTSS in non-institutional settings (4.5 percent). (See figure 3.)

Spending Patterns for Eligibility Groups

The general pattern of greater hospital and LTSS service use by high expenditure Medicaid-only beneficiaries compared with greater spending on managed care and premium support by all other Medicaid-only beneficiaries was consistent across eligibility groups. However, there were some differences in expenditures by eligibility category among high-expenditure Medicaid-only beneficiaries and all other Medicaid-only beneficiaries.

Beneficiary Profile

Beneficiary A was a 61-year-old disabled African American male in 2009, with $73,539 in total Medicaid expenditures in that year. He was not enrolled in managed care at any point in the year. He was indicated to have diabetes, a mental health condition, and resided in a long-term care facility. His expenditures were highly concentrated in LTSS non-institutional care (81.9 percent). About 10 percent of his expenditures were for prescription drugs.

- **Disabled**: For high expenditure Medicaid-only beneficiaries in the disabled category, LTSS non-institutional (27.5 percent), hospital (24.8 percent), and LTSS institutional services (11.9 percent) represent almost two-thirds of their expenditures. (See figure 4.) In contrast, all other Medicaid-only beneficiaries in the disabled category had over half of their expenditures for managed care and premium assistance (52.1 percent), and had almost no LTSS institutional expenditures (0.1 percent). Overall, 79.5 percent of expenditures for Medicaid-only beneficiaries in the disabled group were for the high-expenditure beneficiaries.

Beneficiary Profile

Beneficiary B was a 1-year-old white male in the child eligibility group in 2009, with $90,609 in total Medicaid expenditures in that year. He was not enrolled in managed care, but had costs associated with his delivery. His total expenditures were highly concentrated in hospital services (79.4 percent). About 12 percent of his expenditures were for non-hospital acute care.

- **Children**: Medicaid-only children had almost no LTSS institutional expenditures (less than 1 percent), whether in the high-expenditure group or not.[25] (See figure 5.) High-expenditure Medicaid-only children had 70 percent of their expenditures for hospital (46.1 percent) and LTSS non-institutional services (23.9 percent). For all other Medicaid-only children, over 58 percent of their expenditures were for managed care and premium assistance, followed by non-hospital acute (18.8 percent) and hospital services (9.8 percent).

About 22 percent of expenditures for Medicaid-only children were for those in the high-expenditure group.

BENEFICIARY PROFILE

Beneficiary C was a 21-year-old disabled white female in 2009 with $267,202 in total Medicaid expenditures in that year. She was not enrolled in Medicaid managed care at any point in the year, but was indicated to have a mental health condition, a substance abuse condition, and reside in a long-term care facility. Her expenditures were highly concentrated in hospital services (54.4 percent) and LTSS non-institutional care (30.8 percent).

- **Adults**: Similar to children, Medicaid-only adult beneficiaries had almost no LTSS institutional expenditures (less than 1 percent of each of their total expenditures) whether in the high-expenditure group or not.[26] (See figure 6.) Hospital services represented over half the expenditures for high-expenditure adult beneficiaries. The remaining expenditures were almost equally distributed between non-hospital acute care (15.2 percent), drugs (14.2 percent), and managed care and premium support (14.1 percent). LTSS non-institutional services were a relatively small part of their total expenditures (3.4 percent). The greatest share of expenditures for all other Medicaid-only adult beneficiaries were for managed care and premium support (58.4 percent) followed by hospital (16.2 percent) and non-hospital acute care (15.4 percent) services. About 22 percent of expenditures for Medicaid-only adult beneficiaries were for the high-expenditure group.

BENEFICIARY PROFILE

Beneficiary D was an under 1-year-old disabled male of unknown race in 2009, with $101,225 in total Medicaid expenditures in that year. He was enrolled in Medicaid managed care for 6 to 11 months. He was indicated to have asthma and costs associated with his delivery. His expenditures were highly concentrated in hospital services (84.9 percent). About 9 percent of his expenditures were for non-acute hospital care.

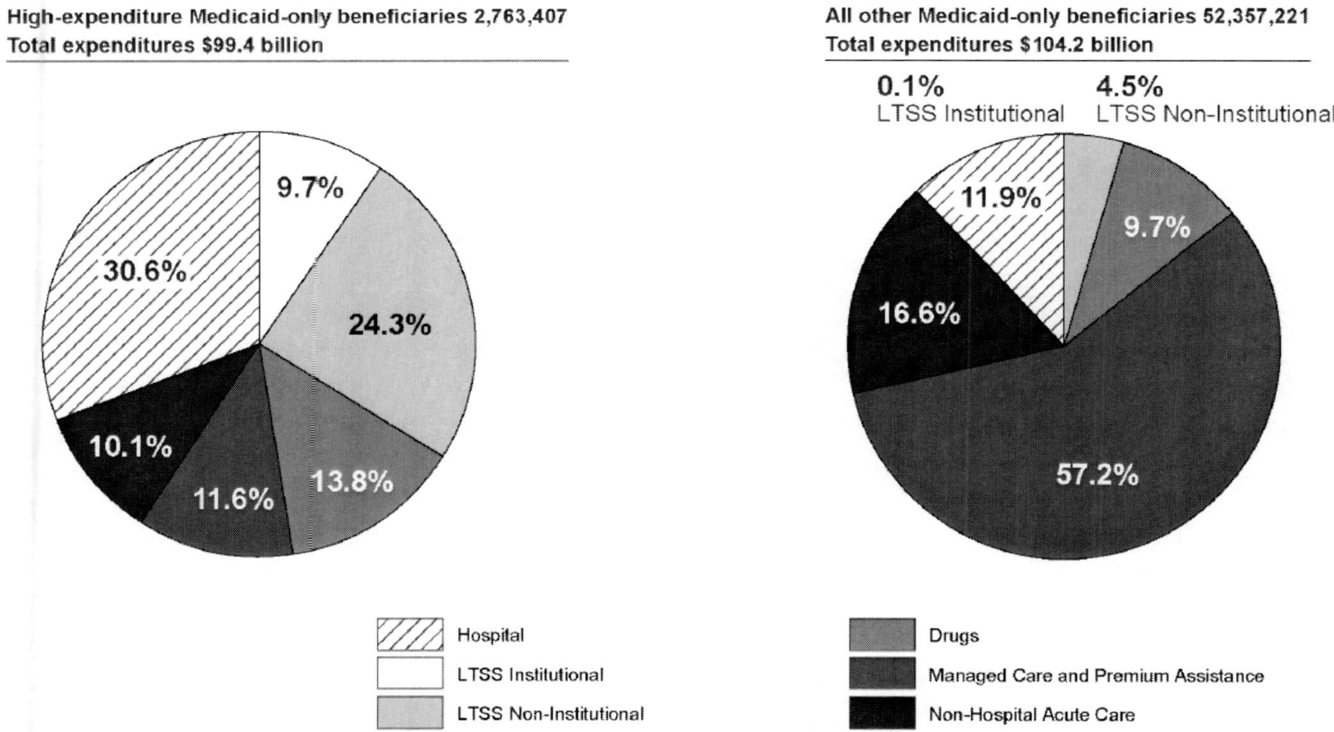

Source: GAO analysis of Centers for Medicare & Medicaid Services data.

Notes: High-expenditure beneficiaries are those whose total expenditures fell within the top 5 percent of total expenditures within each state. All other beneficiaries represent those whose spending was less than the spending for the top 5 percent. Medicaid-only beneficiaries are eligible for Medicaid but not Medicare.

LTSS stands for long-term care services and supports. The spending category managed care and premium assistance includes Medicaid health insurance payments made to risk-based health maintenance organizations, primary care case management services, and prepaid health plans.

Percentages may not add to 100 due to rounding.

Figure 3. Percentage of Expenditures for Services and Managed Care and Premium Assistance for High-Expenditure, and All Other Medicaid-Only Beneficiaries, Fiscal Year 2009.

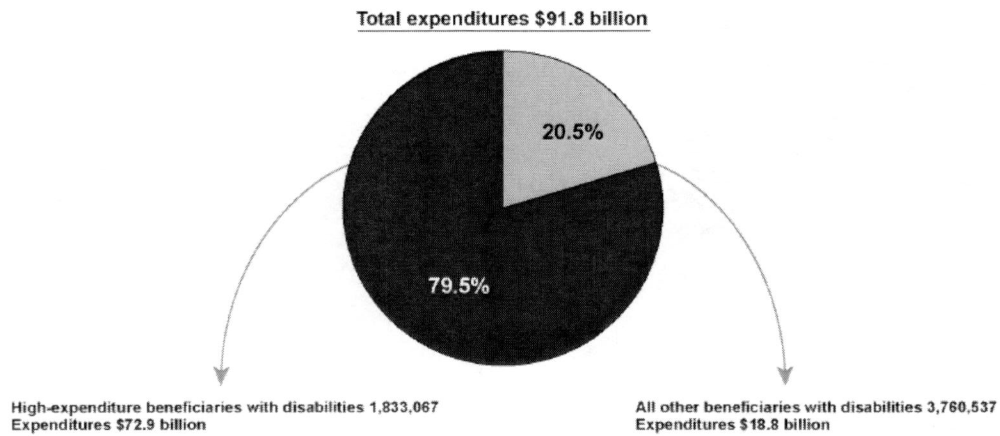

Figure 4. (Continued).

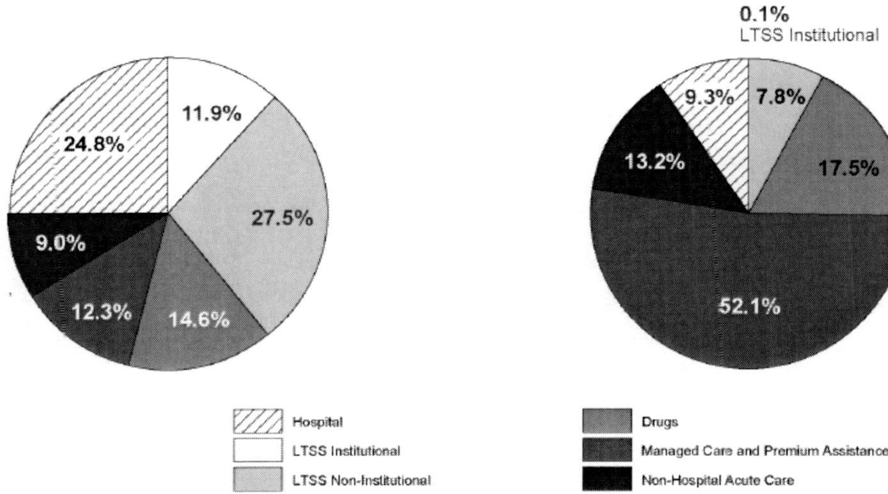

Source: GAO analysis of Centers for Medicare & Medicaid Services data.

Notes: High-expenditure beneficiaries are those whose total expenditures fell within the top 5 percent of total expenditures within each state. All other beneficiaries represent those whose spending was less than the spending for the top 5 percent. Medicaid-only beneficiaries are eligible for Medicaid but not Medicare.

LTSS stands for long-term care services and supports. The spending category managed care and premium assistance includes Medicaid health insurance payments made to risk-based health maintenance organizations, primary care case management services, and prepaid health plans.

Percentages may not add to 100 due to rounding.

Figure 4. Percentage of Expenditures for Services and Managed Care and Premium Assistance for High-Expenditure, and All Other Medicaid-Only Disabled Beneficiaries, Fiscal Year 2009.

- **Aged**: For the aged, both high-expenditure and all other Medicaid-only beneficiaries had LTC institutional expenditures, but the share of those expenditures differed—28.2 percent compared with 4.2 percent. Among the high-expenditure Medicaid-only aged beneficiaries, hospital (28.6 percent), LTSS institutional (28.2 percent), and LTSS non-institutional (15.4 percent) services represented over 70 percent of total expenditures. (See figure7.) For all other Medicaid-only aged beneficiaries, managed care and premium support represented 48.3 percent of their expenditures, followed by drugs (18.2 percent), hospital (13.7 percent), and non-hospital acute care (10.6 percent) services. Over 73 percent of expenditures for the Medicaid-only aged were for those in the high-expenditure group.

Spending Patterns for High-Expenditure Medicaid-Only Beneficiaries by LTC Facility Residence Status

LTSS spending differed for high expenditure Medicaid-only beneficiaries living in LTC facilities and those living in the community. (See figure 8.)

- Among high-expenditure Medicaid-only beneficiaries residing in a LTC facility, expenditures for LTSS in institutional settings (50 percent), hospital services (27.2 percent), and LTSS in non-institutional settings (7.3 percent) accounted for almost 85 percent of their total expenditures.
- Among high-expenditure beneficiaries not residing in a LTC facility, expenditures for LTSS in non-institutional settings (28.4 percent) were much greater, and expenditures for hospital services were similar (31.4 percent)—and these two services represented almost 60 percent of their total expenditures. In addition, the percentage of expenditures on drugs and non-hospital acute care was greater for high expenditure Medicaid-only beneficiaries who were not living in LTC facilities.

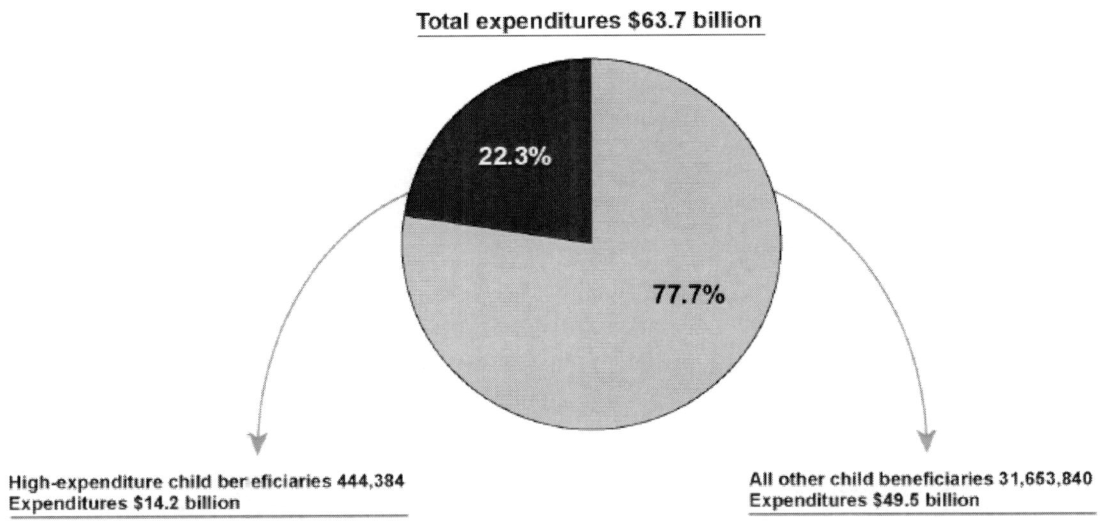

Figure 5. (Continued).

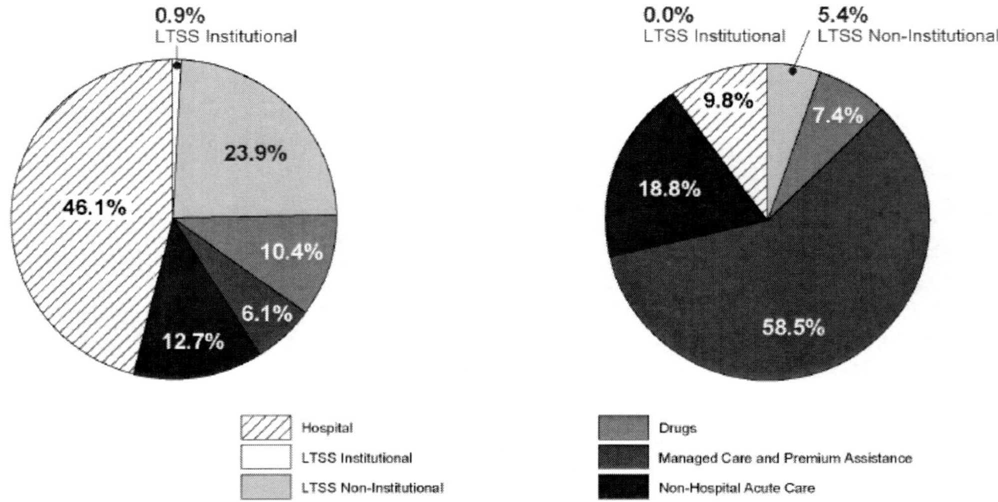

Source: GAO analysis of Centers for Medicare & Medicaid Services data.

Notes: High-expenditure beneficiaries are those whose total expenditures fell within the top 5 percent of total expenditures within each state. All other beneficiaries represent those whose spending was less than the spending for the top 5 percent. Medicaid-only beneficiaries are eligible for Medicaid but not Medicare.

LTSS stands for long-term care services and supports. The spending category managed care and premium assistance includes Medicaid health insurance payments made to risk-based health maintenance organizations, primary care case management services, and prepaid health plans.

Percentages may not add to 100 due to rounding.

Figure 5. Percentage of Expenditures for Services and Managed Care and Premium Assistance for High-Expenditure, and All Other Medicaid-Only Child Beneficiaries, Fiscal Year 2009.

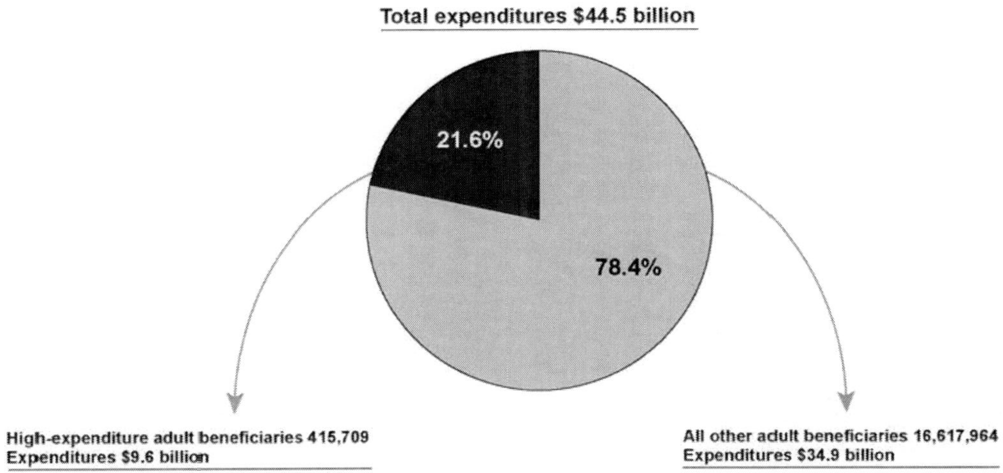

Figure 6. (Continued).

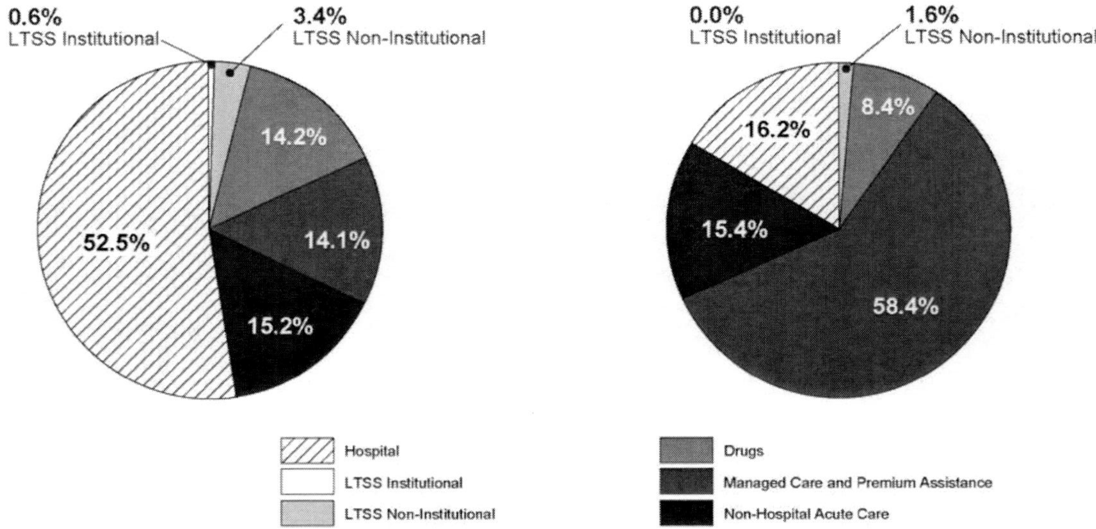

Source: GAO analysis of Centers for Medicare & Medicaid Services data.

Notes: High-expenditure beneficiaries are those whose total expenditures fell within the top 5 percent of total expenditures within each state. All other beneficiaries represent those whose spending was less than the spending for the top 5 percent. Medicaid-only beneficiaries are eligible for Medicaid but not Medicare.

LTSS stands for long-term care services and supports. The spending category managed care and premium assistance includes Medicaid health insurance payments made to risk-based health maintenance organizations, primary care case management services, and prepaid health plans.

Figure 6. Percentage of Expenditures for Services and Managed Care and Premium Assistance for High-Expenditure, and All Other Medicaid-Only Adult Beneficiaries, Fiscal Year 2009.

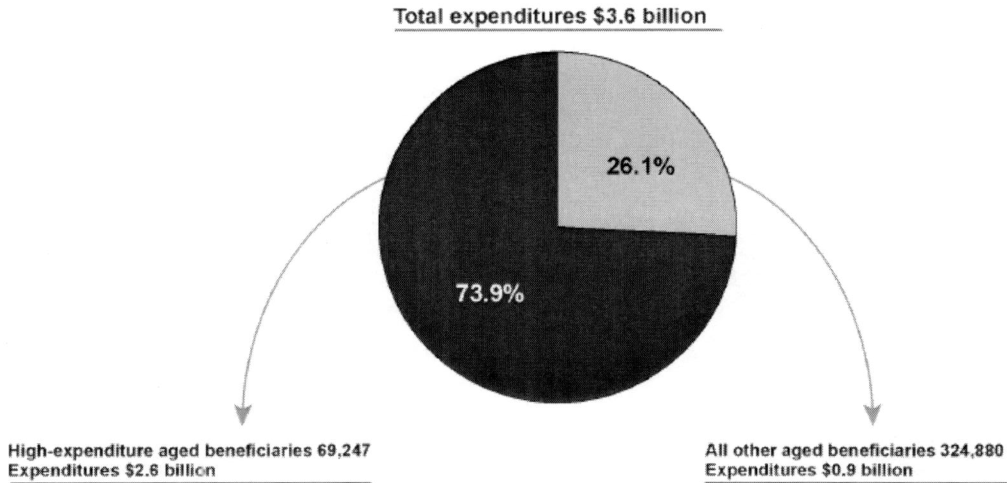

Figure 7. (Continued).

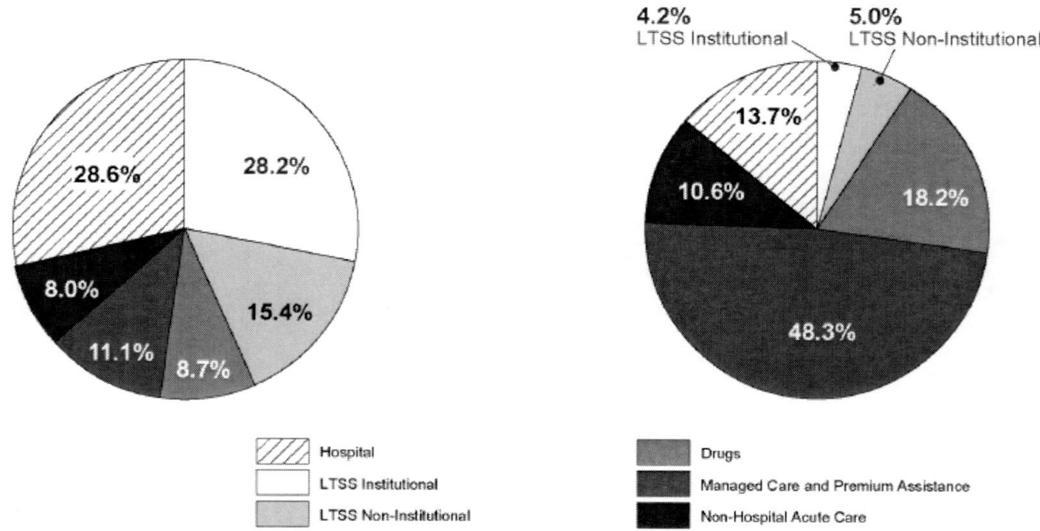

Source: GAO analysis of Centers for Medicare & Medicaid Services data.

Notes: High-expenditure beneficiaries are those whose total expenditures fell within the top 5 percent of total expenditures within each state. All other beneficiaries represent those whose spending was less than the spending for the top 5 percent. Medicaid-only beneficiaries are eligible for Medicaid but not Medicare.

LTSS stands for long-term care services and supports. The spending category managed care and premium assistance includes Medicaid health insurance payments made to risk-based health maintenance organizations, primary care case management services, and prepaid health plans.

Figure 7. Percentage of Expenditures for Services and Managed Care and Premium Assistance for High-Expenditure, and All Other Medicaid-Only Aged Beneficiaries, Fiscal Year 2009.

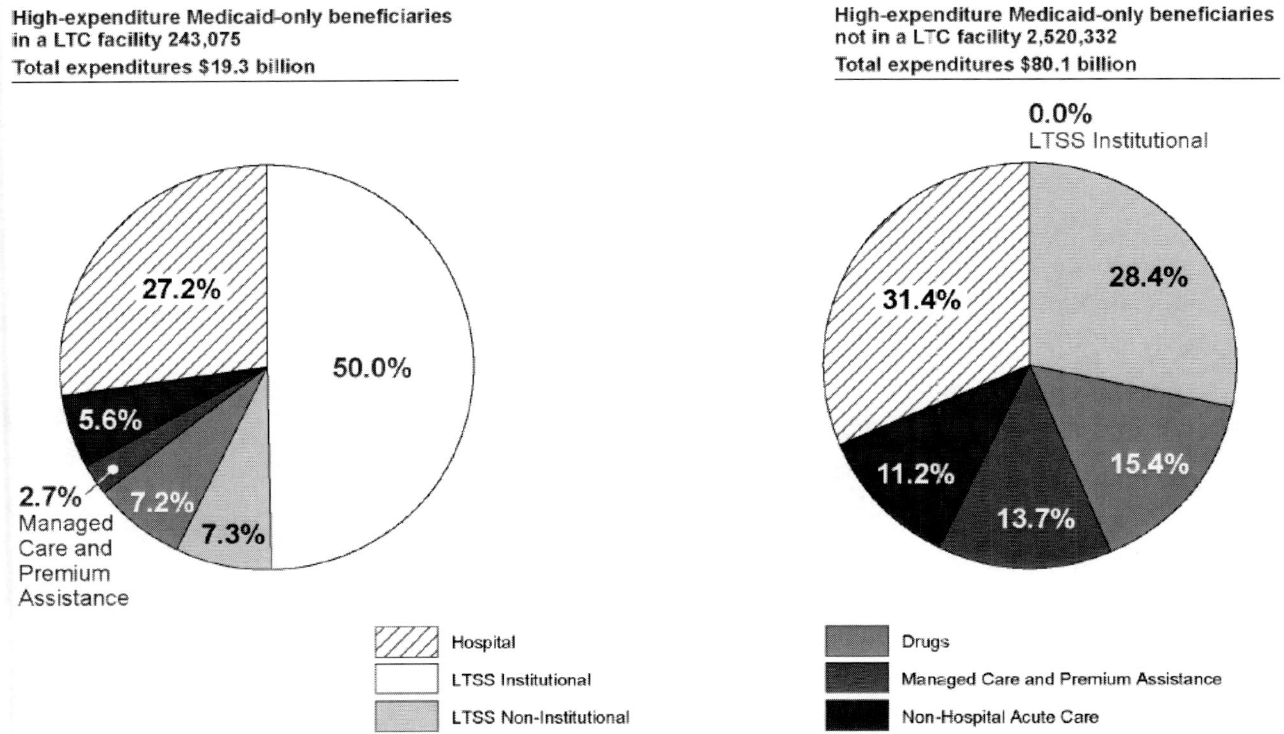

Source: GAO analysis of Centers for Medicare & Medicaid Services data.

Notes: High-expenditure beneficiaries are those whose total expenditures fell within the top 5 percent of total expenditures within each state. All other beneficiaries represent those whose spending was less than the spending for the top 5 percent. Medicaid-only beneficiaries are eligible for Medicaid but not Medicare.

LTC stands for long-term care. LTSS stands for long-term care services and supports. The spending category managed care and premium assistance includes Medicaid health insurance payments made to risk-based health maintenance organizations, primary care case management services, and prepaid health plans.

Percentages may not add to 100 due to rounding.

Figure 8. Percentage of Expenditures for Services and Managed Care and Premium Assistance for High-Expenditure Medicaid-Only Beneficiaries, by Long-Term Care Residence Status, Fiscal Year 2009.

Table 4. Per Capita Expenditures for Services and Managed Care and Premium Assistance for High-Expenditure Medicaid-Only Beneficiaries by Long-Term Care Residence Status, Fiscal Year 2009

	Long-term care facility	No long-term care facility
	Per capita expenditures (dollars)	Per capita expenditures (dollars)
Hospital	21,589	9,978
Non-Hospital Acute Care	4,420	3,543
Drugs	5,738	4,879
Managed Care & Premium Assistance	2,151	4,349
LTSS Non-Institutional	5,833	9,022
LTSS Institutional	39,671	0

Source: GAO analysis of Centers for Medicare & Medicaid Services' data.
Note: LTSS stands for long-term services and supports.

While hospital services were the largest expenditure category among high-expenditure beneficiaries not residing in a LTC facility, per-capita hospital expenditures for beneficiaries residing in a LTC facility were over two times as much ($21,589 compared with $9,978). (See table 4.)

Spending Patterns for Beneficiaries in the Top 1 Percent of Expenditures

Beneficiaries with expenditures within the top 1 percent for their state—the top one-fifth of the high-expenditure group—had a greater share of spending on hospital services, LTSS in non-institutional settings, and LTSS in institutional settings compared with all of the high-expenditure beneficiaries. Spending on these services comprised almost 80 percent of the total expenditures for beneficiaries with expenditures within the top 1 percent for their state. (See app. IV for complete table of results, and app. V for the demographic characteristics and spending for some randomly selected beneficiaries in that group.)

Agency Comments

HHS reviewed a draft of this report and provided technical comments, which we incorporated as appropriate.

Sincerely yours,

Carolyn L. Yocom
Director, Health Care

Appendix I. Objectives, Scope, and Methodology

This appendix describes the methodology for addressing three objectives that examine: (1) states' spending for high-expenditure beneficiaries, both Medicaid-only and dual-eligible beneficiaries, compared with other Medicaid beneficiaries; (2) the characteristics associated with high- expenditure Medicaid-only beneficiaries; and (3) the services that contributed to high expenditures for Medicaid-only beneficiaries, and how they compared with service usage by all other Medicaid-only beneficiaries.

We analyzed data from the fiscal year 2009 Medicaid Statistical Information System (MSIS) Annual Person Summary File.[27] The summary file consolidates individual beneficiaries' claims for the fiscal year, including data on their enrollment and information on their expenditures. The summary file also includes beneficiary specific information regarding enrollment categories, expenditures among six categories,[28] dual eligibility status, age, gender, payment arrangements—including fee-for-service payments and capitated payments made to managed care organizations—and indicators for five conditions and two service categories.[29] The summary file excludes some encounter details included in the full claims files (for example, the summary file may not include details regarding the care encounter, such as individual cost per encounter; however, it does include monthly enrollment data).

We made several adjustments to the summary file in order to ensure that the data were reliable for our purposes. Specifically we excluded:

- records with unknown eligibility status (eliminated 5,166,648 records, or 7.21 percent of total records);

- all records associated with duplicate MSIS IDs or Social Security numbers within a state (eliminated 277,363 records, or 0.39 percent of total records);
- records with negative total spending amounts (eliminated 975,869 records, or 1.36 percent of total records), which may reflect adjustments to claims made in the prior year;
- records of individuals who were only enrolled in a stand-alone, separate Children's Health Insurance Program during the year (eliminated 471,507 records, or 0.66 percent of total records);
- records associated with a payment adjustment rather than an individual (eliminated 202,456 records, or 0.28 percent of total records);
- records of individuals whose age appeared to conflict with their identified eligibility group (eliminated 65,016 records, or 0.09 percent of total records). For example, records of individuals in the child eligibility group whose age was 85 and older;
- records with unknown dual status (eliminated 698 records, or less than 0.01 percent of total records); and,
- records of individuals whose age was over 65, but indicated as having delivered a child (eliminated 126 records, or less than 0.01 percent of total records).

After making these adjustments, we were able to retain 64,457,343, or 90 percent, of the summary file's 71,617,026 original records.

In order to determine variations in states' spending for high-expenditure Medicaid-only beneficiaries compared with other Medicaid beneficiaries, we calculated the total number of Medicaid enrollees and total Medicaid expenditures in each state. We then calculated these same statistics for our subpopulations of Medicaid-only and dual-eligible beneficiaries based on the "last-best" indicator of dual eligibility status available in the summary file. Medicaid-only beneficiaries were eligible for Medicaid but not Medicare. Dual-eligible beneficiaries were eligible for both Medicaid and Medicare. Next, we determined the number of beneficiaries whose total expenditures fell within the top 5 percent of total expenditures within each state (we calculated these figures separately for Medicaid-only and dual-eligible beneficiaries). We termed these 2,763,407 beneficiaries as high-expenditure beneficiaries. We then separately calculated the total expenditures for our high-expenditure beneficiaries and other beneficiaries in each state for Medicaid-only and dual-eligible beneficiaries, and summed this data at a national level.

To examine the characteristics associated with high-expenditure Medicaid-only beneficiaries, we determined the percentage of high-expenditure Medicaid-only beneficiaries with key characteristics and used logistic regression to examine the effect of having key beneficiary characteristics on the probability of being a high-expenditure Medicaid- only beneficiary. The key beneficiary characteristics for which we describe the high-expenditure beneficiary population and represented as independent variables in our logistic regression model included: eligibility group (disabled, child, adult, aged), age, gender, race/ethnicity, geographic location,[30] participation in capitated managed care,[31] period of enrollment in Medicaid (whether full year or partial year), as well as whether the beneficiaries had any of five health conditions or had received any of two services. Finally, our logistic regression models included characteristics of states' Medicaid programs, including their spending on high-expenditure beneficiaries and long-term services and supports (LTSS) in non-institutional settings (also called home and community based services) and capitated managed care penetration rates.[32] We report percentages that describe the high-expenditure beneficiary population, as well as the probabilities that demonstrate the association of each characteristic with the likelihood of being in the high-expenditure group if all beneficiaries had a particular characteristic while holding all other characteristics constant. Probabilities were calculated by converting the odds that resulted from our logistic regression models. The size of the independent effect of each enrollee characteristic is expressed as a probability, with greater values reflecting a greater chance that the characteristic increased the likelihood of being a high-expenditure beneficiary. Medicaid-only beneficiaries had a hypothetical 5 percent probability of being in the high-expenditure group by chance alone. All probabilities were significant at the 0.05 level.

In order to determine which service categories contributed to expenditures for high-expenditure Medicaid-only beneficiaries, we examined how total expenditures for high-expenditure Medicaid-only beneficiaries were distributed among the following six expenditure categories: (1) hospital care, (2) non-hospital acute care, (3) drugs, (4) managed care and premium assistance, (5) long-term services and supports (LTSS) in non-institutional settings, and (6) long-term services and supports in institutional settings.[33] We then examined the distribution of spending among each of the six expenditure categories for beneficiaries in our high-expenditure group compared to the distribution of spending among each of the six expenditure categories for all other Medicaid-only beneficiaries.

We conducted this performance audit from September 2012 through February 2014 in accordance with generally accepted government auditing standards. Those standards require that we plan and perform the audit to obtain sufficient, appropriate evidence to provide a reasonable basis for our findings and conclusions based on our audit objectives. We believe that the evidence obtained provides a reasonable basis for our findings and conclusions based on our audit objectives.

APPENDIX II. CHARACTERISTICS OF HIGH- EXPENDITURE MEDICAID-ONLY BENEFICIARIES

The table below demonstrates the characteristics of high-expenditure Medicaid-only beneficiaries, and how expenditures were distributed within each characteristic of interest. For each subpopulation, we also calculated the per-capita expenditures in dollars. High-expenditure Medicaid-only beneficiaries who resided in a long-term care (LTC) facility during fiscal year 2009 had the highest per capita expenditures ($79,464).

Table 5. Characteristics of High-Expenditure Medicaid-Only Beneficiaries (Top 5 Percent of Expenditures), Fiscal Year 2009

	Beneficiaries (percent)	Expenditures (percent)	Per capita expenditures (dollars)
Overall	100	100	35,983
Eligibility Group			
Children	16.1	14.3	32,005
Adults	15.0	9.6	23,064
Disabled	66.3	73.4	39,799
Aged	2.5	2.7	38,112
Age			
Under 1	2.8	3.8	48,069
1-21	31.1	30.4	35,177
22-44	28.3	28.2	35,942
45-64	34.6	34.1	35,465
65-84	2.8	3.0	38,705

Table 5. (Continued)

	Beneficiaries (percent)	Expenditures (percent)	Per capita expenditures (dollars)
85 & Over	0.4	0.5	40,422
Gender			
Female	55.1	49.5	32,368
Male	44.9	50.5	40,404
Race/Ethnicity			
White	45.7	45.9	36,110
Black or African American	23.9	24.6	37,089
American Indian or Alaska Native	1.7	1.7	37,345
Asian	2.0	1.9	33,638
Hispanic or Latino (includes Hispanic or Latino with 1+ races)	16.6	14.8	32,136
Native Hawaiian or other Pacific Islander	1.1	0.8	27,468
More than one race	0.2	0.4	53,682
Capitated Managed Care			
12 months	25.3	16.0	22,780
6-11 months	8.2	6.0	26,462
1-5 months	5.2	5.2	35,900
0 months	61.4	72.8	42,703
Length of Medicaid Coverage			
Partial-year coverage	11.5	12.0	37,630
Full-year coverage	88.5	88.0	35,769
Metropolitan Status			
Metropolitan counties	79.5	78.8	35,674
Nonmetropolitan counties	17.6	16.9	34,615
Condition and Services			
HIV/AIDS	3.4	4.4	45,825
Asthma	14.5	15.4	38,324
Diabetes	18.6	20.5	39,642
Delivery/Childbirth	9.8	8.0	29,227
Mental health	51.8	55.2	38,374
Substance abuse	19.1	19.3	36,302
Long-term care residence	8.8	19.4	79,464

Source: GAO analysis of Centers for Medicare & Medicaid Services' data.

Notes: High-expenditure beneficiaries represent those whose total expenditures fell within the top 5 percent of total expenditures within each state. Medicaid-only beneficiaries are eligible for Medicaid but not Medicare.

Capitated managed care includes enrollment in a health maintenance organization or capitated risk- based managed care plans. Limited benefit plans were excluded from this analysis.

HIV/AIDS stands for human immunodeficiency virus/acquired immunodeficiency syndrome. Delivery/childbirth may include costs attributed to a mother during delivery or the child soon after birth.

Percentages may not add to 100 due to missing or unknown data.

Appendix III. Key Characteristics Associated with Estimated Probability of being a High-Expenditure Beneficiary

Our logistic regression analysis found that key characteristics—such as having a disability, having certain conditions, delivery/childbirth, and residing in a LTC facility—were consistently strongly associated with being a high-expenditure Medicaid-only beneficiary when looking at all records, and when the data was examined separately for each eligibility group.

Table 6. Estimated Probability of being a High-Expenditure Medicaid-Only Beneficiary (Full Model Results), by Selected Conditions and Services, Fiscal Year 2009

Probability (Percent)					
	(1) All Records	(2) Children	(3) Adults	(4) Aged	(5) Disabled
Eligibility Group					
Children	2.0	N/A[a]	N/A	N/A	N/A
Adult	2.6	N/A	N/A	N/A	N/A
Disabled	18.3	N/A	N/A	N/A	N/A
Aged	10.5	N/A	N/A	N/A	N/A
Age					
Under <1	7.7	N/A	N/A	N/A	63.7
1-21	5.4	N/A	N/A	N/A	35.9

Table 6. (Continued)

	(1) All Records	(2) Children	(3) Adults	(4) Aged	(5) Disabled
22-44	5.9	N/A	N/A	N/A	39.9
45-64	6.8	N/A	N/A	N/A	41.2
65-84	6.8	N/A	N/A	N/A	40.7
85 & over	7.0	N/A	N/A	N/A	32.7
Gender					
Males	5.1	1.5	2.6	17.6	32.5
Females	4.9	1.3	2.4	16.6	32.8
Race/Ethnicity					
White	4.9	1.5	2.5	16.2	31.7
Black or African American	4.5	1.6	2.7	17.7	27.0
Hispanic or Latino (includes Hispanic or Latino with 1+ races)	4.5	1.5	2.4	13.4	30.7
Asian	4.4	1.4	2.2	12.2	35.0
American Indian or Alaska Native	6.8	2.7	4.7	16.1	33.3
Native Hawaiian or other Pacific Islander	4.2	1.5	2.9	11.6	27.5
More than one race	4.2	1.4	2.2	11.5	27.1
Unknown	4.3	1.6	2.3	12.0	28.8
Capitated Managed Care					
12 months	4.9	0.9	1.5	15.0	36.9
6-11 months	3.8	0.9	2.0	12.3	24.7
1-5 months	4.3	1.3	2.5	13.6	24.9
0 months	5.4	2.0	3.2	18.1	32.3
Length of Medicaid Coverage					
Partial-year coverage	2.9	0.8	1.4	9.1	18.4
Full-year coverage	5.6	1.6	3.2	21.7	34.9
Metropolitan Status					
Metropolitan counties	5.1	1.4	2.4	17.3	33.2
Non-metropolitan counties	4.6	1.2	2.5	13.5	30.5
Condition and Services					
HIV/AIDS	20.8	11.4	23.9	41.2	71.6
No HIV/AIDS	4.9	1.4	2.3	16.9	32.1
Asthma	6.8	2.3	4.4	29.7	39.4

	(1) All Records	(2) Children	(3) Adults	(4) Aged	(5) Disabled
No asthma	4.8	1.3	2.3	16.4	31.8
Delivery/childbirth	13.3	8.2	8.9	17.0	46.7
No delivery/childbirth	4.6	1.1	1.8	17.0	32.5
Diabetic	8.8	5.9	7.7	26.3	47.1
Not diabetic	4.6	1.4	2.2	14.2	30.3
Long-term care	24.2	11.6	8.6	53.9	82.1
Not long-term care	4.7	1.3	2.4	14.0	31.0
Mental health conditions	9.1	7.0	5.4	32.0	42.4
No mental health conditions	3.7	0.7	1.9	14.7	26.4
Substance abuse	7.9	3.5	6.3	30.2	42.7
No substance abuse	4.7	1.3	2.0	16.7	31.2
State Characteristics					
State's HMO penetration in Q1	4.2	1.0	1.5	21.7	30.3
State's HMO penetration in Q2	4.3	1.4	1.7	16.6	27.1
State's HMO penetration in Q3	5.3	1.3	2.8	24.1	35.1
State's HMO penetration in Q4	5.5	1.8	2.9	14.5	35.1
State's Medicaid spending in Q1	4.6	1.0	1.7	16.3	31.5
State's Medicaid spending in Q2	5.1	1.5	2.4	17.3	33.7
State's Medicaid spending in Q3	4.5	1.3	2.7	12.9	27.4
State's Medicaid spending in Q4	5.8	1.6	3.1	20.4	39.2
State home and community-based services spending in Q1	4.7	1.5	4.0	14.0	27.6
State home and community-based services spending in Q2	5.3	1.3	2.6	17.1	36.3
State home and community-based services spending in Q3	5.1	1.7	2.1	17.0	32.8
State home and community-based services spending in Q4	4.4	0.9	1.9	18.3	32.0

Source: GAO analysis of Centers for Medicare & Medicaid Services' data.

Notes: High-expenditure beneficiaries represent those whose total expenditures fell within the top 5 percent of total expenditures within each state. All other beneficiaries represent those whose spending was less than the spending for the top 5 percent. Medicaid-only beneficiaries are eligible for Medicaid but not Medicare.

Probabilities are derived from logistic regression results. Medicaid-only beneficiaries had a hypothetical 5 percent probability of being in the high-expenditure group by chance alone. A probability less than 5 percent indicates that a characteristic's influence on the beneficiary's being in the high-expenditure group was less than what would have occurred by chance alone, while probabilities greater than 5 percent indicate the opposite. All probabilities were significant at the 0.05 level.

The probabilities in each column are derived from logistic regressions that used different samples and are therefore inappropriate for cross comparison.

Capitated managed care includes enrollment in a health maintenance organization (HMO) or capitated risk-based managed care plans. Limited benefit plans were excluded from this analysis.

HIV/AIDS stands for human immunodeficiency virus/acquired immunodeficiency syndrome. Q stands for quarter of the fiscal year.

Delivery/childbirth may include costs attributed to a mother during delivery or the child soon after birth.

State spending on high-expenditure Medicaid-only beneficiaries uses information on the distribution of expenditures for the Medicaid-only group and separates states by quartiles. The variable for state spending on home and community-based services divides the total Medicaid expenditures for home and community-based services by expenditures for all Medicaid beneficiaries, and separates states into quartiles. The state managed care penetration variable of data on HMO penetration rates by state also separates states by quartiles.

[a] Not included in model.

Appendix IV. Characteristics of High-Expenditure Beneficiaries in the Top 1 Percent of Expenditures

The table below demonstrates the characteristics of Medicaid-only beneficiaries with expenditures in the top 1 percent of total expenditures (558,798 beneficiaries). For each subpopulation, we also calculated the per capita expenditures in dollars. The top 1 percent of Medicaid-only beneficiaries had per capita spending of $94,821, over 2.5 times that of beneficiaries in the top 5 percent of total expenditures whose per capita spending was $35,983 (top 1 percent included).

Table 7. Characteristics of High-Expenditure Medicaid-Only Beneficiaries (Top 1 Percent of Expenditures), Fiscal Year 2009

	Beneficiaries (percent)	Expenditures (percent)	Per capita expenditures (dollars)
Overall	100	100	94,821
Eligibility Category			
Children	11.8	12.4	99,588
Adults	5.3	4.7	83,809
Disabled	79.8	80.2	95,279
Aged	3.1	2.7	83,621
Age			
Under 1	4.0	4.8	113,685
1-21	28.2	29.9	100,686
22-44	28.2	29.2	97,910
45-64	35.4	32.4	86,746
65-84	3.6	3.3	85,610
85 & Over	0.6	0.5	76,137
Gender			
Female	47.3	44.8	89,842
Male	52.7	55.1	99,268
Race/Ethnicity			
White	47.7	45.8	91,141
Black or African American	23.4	24.2	97,848
American Indian or Alaska Native	1.7	1.7	94,123
Asian	1.9	1.8	89,060
Hispanic or Latino (includes Hispanic or Latino with 1+ races)	14.0	14.2	95,667
Native Hawaiian or other Pacific Islander	1.0	0.9	82,900
More than one race	0.2	0.4	171,292
Capitated Managed Care			
12 months	10.5	8.3	75,519
6-11 months	4.8	4.2	82,202
1-5 months	5.2	5.1	92,982
0 months	79.5	82.4	98,245

Table 7. (Continued)

	Beneficiaries (percent)	Expenditures (percent)	Per capita expenditures (dollars)
Length of Medicaid Coverage			
Partial-year coverage	12.1	12.3	97,035
Full-year coverage	88.0	87.7	94,518
Metropolitan Status			
Metropolitan counties	80.5	79.4	93,582
Non-metropolitan counties	16.6	15.5	88,696
Condition and Service Flags			
HIV/AIDS	4.0	4.2	98,379
Asthma	14.7	15.5	99,783
Diabetes	22.4	21.9	92,790
Delivery	6.4	7.5	110,078
Mental health	56.7	56.5	94,468
Substance abuse	18.2	17.2	89,500
Long-term care residence	26.0	30.8	112,528
Expenditure Categories			
Hospital		34.8	32,967
Non-hospital acute care		7.6	7,157
Drugs		9.8	9,326
Managed care & premium assistance		4.6	4,402
LTSS non-institutional		26.4	25,043
LTSS institutional		16.7	15,849

Source: GAO analysis of Centers for Medicare & Medicaid Services' data.

Notes: The top 1 percent of beneficiaries represent those whose total expenditures fell within the top 1 percent of total expenditures within each state. Medicaid-only beneficiaries are eligible for Medicaid but not Medicare. However, Medicaid-only beneficiaries may have other sources of health care coverage.

Capitated managed care includes enrollment in a health maintenance organization or capitated risk- based managed care plans. Limited benefit plans were excluded from this analysis.

HIV/AIDS stands for human immunodeficiency virus/acquired immunodeficiency syndrome.

Delivery/childbirth may include costs attributed to a mother during delivery or the child soon after birth.

Percentages may not add to 100 due to missing or unknown data.

APPENDIX V. SELECTED CASES OF MEDICAID-ONLY BENEFICIARIES WITH EXPENDITURES IN THE TOP 1 PERCENT

We examined individual cases of a random group of Medicaid-only beneficiaries in the top 1 percent of expenditures. Some of these beneficiaries illustrated the trends identified in our analysis, but we also found beneficiaries who demonstrated that there was diversity among the high-expenditure group. Below are some examples of the characteristics and spending patterns for individual beneficiaries. Overall, per capita spending in the top 1 percent ranged from $19,068 to $43,728,641, with an average expenditure of $94,821.

Table 8. Characteristics of Selected Cases of Medicaid-Only Beneficiaries with Expenditures in the Top 1 Percent, Fiscal Year 2009

Beneficiary	Eligibility category	Conditions and/or services	HMO/capitated risk-based managed care enrollment	Total expenditures in 2009 (dollars)	Largest expenditure category
74-year-old black or African American male	Aged	None	None	142,809	95.3 percent hospital
55-year-old black or African American male	Disabled	Diabetes, mental health, substance abuse, LTC residence	None	107,182	44.9 percent LTSS institutional
Under 1-year-old white female	Child	Mental health	None	91,314	84.5 percent hospital
85-year-old black or African American male	Aged	Diabetes, mental health, LTC residence	None	71,346	84.6 percent LTSS institutional

Table 8. (Continued)

Beneficiary	Eligibility category	Conditions and/or services	HMO/capitated risk-based managed care enrollment	Total expenditures in 2009 (dollars)	Largest expenditure category
57-year-old white male	Disabled	Diabetes, substance abuse	None	57,719	76.3 percent LTSS non-institutional
15-year-old Hispanic or Latino female	Disabled	Mental health	12 months	55,736	65.1 percent LTSS non-institutional
7-year-old male, race unknown	Disabled	None	12 months	46,153	81 percent prescription drugs
3-year-old white male	Disabled	Mental health	None	42,027	100 percent managed care and premium assistance
40-year-old Hispanic or Latino female	Adult	None	1-5 months	39,182	87 percent non-hospital acute care
52-year-old white female	Adult	Asthma, mental health	None	20,363	54.2 percent prescription drugs

Source: GAO analysis of Centers for Medicare & Medicaid Services' data.

Note: The top 1 percent of beneficiaries represent those whose total expenditures fell within the top 1 percent of total expenditures within each state. Medicaid-only beneficiaries are eligible for Medicaid but not Medicare. However, Medicaid-only beneficiaries may have other sources of health care coverage.

Capitated managed care includes enrollment in a health maintenance organization (HMO) or capitated risk-based managed care plans.

Limited benefit plans were excluded from this analysis.

LTSS stands for long-term services and supports.

End Notes

[1] The expansion will apply to Americans with incomes at or below 138 percent of the federal poverty level (FPL), including previously ineligible categories, such as childless adults. PPACA established 133 percent of the FPL as the income limit for expanded Medicaid eligibility; however, it also specified that an income disregard in the amount of 5 percent of the FPL be deducted from an individual's income when determining Medicaid eligibility, which effectively raised the eligibility limit for newly eligible Medicaid recipients to 138 percent of the FPL. Pub. L. No. 111-148, 124 Stat. 119, as amended by the Health Care and Education Reconciliation Act of 2010 (HCERA), Pub. L. No. 111-152, 124 Stat. 1029. For purposes of this report, references to PPACA include the amendments made by HCERA.

[2] CHIP is an insurance program for certain low-income, uninsured children whose family income is too high for Medicaid. Congressional Budget Office, *Estimates for the Insurance Coverage Provisions of the Affordable Care Act Updated for the Recent Supreme Court Decision* (Washington, D.C.: July 2012).

[3] Medicare is the federally financed health insurance program for persons aged 65 and over, certain individuals with disabilities, and individuals with end-stage renal disease.

[4] MSIS data provides a summary of expenditures linked to specific beneficiaries on the basis of their medical claims for care. These data exclude other aspects of the Medicaid program that are not tied to specific beneficiaries. For example, the MSIS data do not contain supplemental payments to providers that are separate from standard Medicaid payments for services.

[5] We excluded individuals who were only enrolled in a stand-alone, separate Children's Health Insurance Program during the year.

[6] Probabilities were calculated by converting the odds that resulted from our logistic regression models. The size of the effect of each enrollee characteristic is expressed as a probability, greater values reflecting a greater chance that the characteristic increased the likelihood of being a high-expenditure beneficiary. Medicaid-only beneficiaries had a hypothetical 5 percent probability of being in the high-expenditure group by chance alone. All probabilities were significant at the 0.05 level.

[7] We classified counties as metropolitan or nonmetropolitan using the 2009 Area Resource File provided by the Health Resources and Services Administration.

[8] Capitated managed care included enrollment in a health maintenance organization (HMO) or capitated risk-based managed care plans. We did not consider enrollment in limited benefit plans as an indicator of this beneficiary characteristic.

[9] The five conditions identified in the MSIS summary file (using indicators created with the ICD-9 diagnosis codes from the full claims file) are: (1) human immunodeficiency virus/acquired immunodeficiency syndrome (HIV/AIDS), (2) asthma, (3) diabetes, (4) mental health, and (5) substance abuse. The two service categories also identified are delivery/childbirth, which includes newborns and women who have given birth, and long-term care residence. The summary file does not provide information on all conditions that may affect the likelihood of the beneficiary being a high-expenditure Medicaid-only beneficiary. As a result, we could not include all relevant conditions in our models.

[10] LTSS includes services such as home health and personal care. We created variables on state spending on high-expenditure Medicaid-only beneficiaries using information from MSIS on the percent of expenditures for the Medicaid-only group and separating states by quartiles. We created variables for state spending on home and community-based services by dividing the total Medicaid expenditures for these services by expenditures for all Medicaid services and separating states into quartiles. We obtained data for state spending on home and community-based services from MSIS and Kaiser Family Foundation, *Medicaid Home and Community-Based Services: 2009 Data Update* (Washington, D.C.: December 2012). We created variables for state managed care penetration using data on the percentage of

individuals covered by HMO and other risk- based capitated managed care (HMO penetration rates) by state and separating states by quartiles. We obtained data for this variable from GAO, *Medicaid: States' Use of Managed Care*, GAO-12-872R (Washington, D.C.: Aug. 17, 2012).

[11] Managed care and premium assistance describe Medicaid health insurance payments made toward HMO/capitated risk-based, primary care case management, and prepaid managed care health plans.

[12] Includes facilities such as skilled nursing facilities and intermediate care facilities for persons with intellectual disabilities.

[13] GAO, Medicaid: Data Sets Provide Inconsistent Picture of Expenditures, GAO-13-47 (Washington, D.C.: Oct. 29, 2012).

[14] Kaiser Family Foundation, *Medicaid's Role in Meeting the Long Term Care Needs of America's Seniors* (Washington, D.C.: January 2013).

[15] GAO, Medicaid: States' Use of Managed Care, GAO-12-872R (Washington, D.C.: Aug. 17, 2012).

[16] Kaiser Family Foundation, *A Profile of Medicaid Managed Care Programs in 2010: Findings from a 50-State Survey* (Washington, D.C.: September 2011).

[17] Kaiser Family Foundation, *Medicaid's Role for Dual Eligible Beneficiaries* (Washington, D.C., August 2013).

[18] Full benefit dual-eligible beneficiaries may receive the entire range of Medicaid benefits as opposed to partial dual-eligible beneficiaries. Partial dual-eligible beneficiaries may receive assistance for covering Medicare premiums, cost-sharing, or both. Medicaid and CHIP Payment and Access Commission, *Report to the Congress on Medicaid and CHIP* (Washington, D.C.: March 2013).

[19] Intermediate care included intermediate care facility services for persons with intellectual disabilities, services in institutions for mental disease for the elderly, and inpatient psychiatric care under age 21. Kaiser Family Foundation, *Medicaid's High Cost Enrollees* (Washington, D.C.: March 2006).

[20] Center for Health Care Strategy, Inc., *Clarifying Multimorbidity Patterns to Improve Targeting and Delivery of Clinical Services for Medicaid Populations* (Hamilton, N.J.: December 2010).

[21] Figures include beneficiaries with restricted benefits, such as those who only receive family planning benefits.

[22] Delivery/childbirth may include costs attributed to a mother during delivery or the child soon after birth.

[23] Some individuals with a disability may be enrolled in Medicaid under other eligibility groups. For example, in some states, children with disabilities may be assigned to an eligibility group based on their age and not their disability status. Our analysis of beneficiaries who resided in a long-term care facility found that 15.3 percent were in the eligibility group for children, while 74.3 percent were in the disabled eligibility group, and the rest were in the aged or adult eligibility groups.

[24] Characteristics of the state included state spending on high-expenditure Medicaid-only beneficiaries, state spending on home and community based services, and state managed care penetration rates.

[25] This suggests that states are generally classifying beneficiaries aged 21 and under who need institutional care as disabled. Our data shows that 27.8 percent of beneficiaries receiving LTSS institutional care were aged 21 and under.

[26] This suggests that states are generally classifying individuals of adult age who need institutional care as disabled. Our data shows that 18.3 percent of beneficiaries receiving LTSS institutional care were aged 22 to 44, and 44 percent were aged 45 to 64.

[27] MSIS data provide a summary of expenditures linked to specific beneficiaries on the basis of their medical claims for care. These data exclude other aspects of the Medicaid program that are not tied to specific beneficiaries. For example, the MSIS data do not contain

supplemental payments to providers that are separate from standard Medicaid payments for services.

[28] The summary file includes information on spending for 30 types of services. We consolidated 28 of these types of services into the six categories we report:(1) hospital care, (2) non-hospital acute care, (3) drugs, (4) managed care and premium assistance, (5) long-term services and supports in non-institutional settings, and (6) long-term services and supports in institutional settings. The summary file does not provide information on all conditions that may affect the likelihood of the beneficiary being a high-expenditure Medicaid-only beneficiary. As a result, we could not include all relevant conditions in our models.

[29] The five chronic condition indicators are for human immunodeficiency virus/acquired immunodeficiency syndrome (HIV/AIDS), mental health issues, diabetes, substance abuse, and asthma. The two service category indicators are for delivery/childbirth and long-term care residency. Childbirth may include costs attributed to a mother during delivery or the child soon after birth. We reviewed the algorithms the indicators were based on by looking up the ICD-9 codes indicated and, where possible, comparing them to codes included in CMS's Chronic Condition Data Warehouse indicators. We determined that despite small differences with the Chronic Condition Data Warehouse (e.g., MSIS did not include secondary diabetes diagnoses) they were sufficient for our purposes.

[30] We classified counties as metropolitan or nonmetropolitan using the 2009 Area Resource File provided by the Health Resources and Services Administration.

[31] Capitated managed care included enrollment in a HMO or capitated risk-based managed care plans. We did not consider enrollment in limited benefit plans as an indicator of this beneficiary characteristic.

[32] LTSS includes services such as home health and personal care. We created variables on state spending on high-expenditure Medicaid-only beneficiaries using information from MSIS on the percent of expenditures for the Medicaid-only group and separating states by quartiles. We created variables for state spending on home and community-based services by dividing the total Medicaid expenditures for these services by expenditures for all Medicaid services and separating states into quartiles. We obtained data for state spending on home and community-based services from MSIS and Kaiser Family Foundation, *Medicaid Home and Community-Based Services: 2009 Data Update* (Washington, D.C.: December 2012). We created variables for state managed care penetration using data on the percentage of individuals covered by HMO and other risk- based capitated managed care (HMO penetration rates) by state and separating states by quartiles. We obtained data for this variable from GAO, *Medicaid: States' Use of Managed Care*, GAO-12-872R (Washington, D.C.: Aug. 17, 2012).

[33] The summary file includes information on spending for 30 types of services. We consolidated 28 of these types of services into the six categories we report.

In: Disproportionate Medicaid Expenditures ISBN: 978-1-63321-118-6
Editor: Cassie Pavesi

Chapter 2

MEDICAID DISPROPORTIONATE SHARE HOSPITAL PAYMENTS*

Alison Mitchell

SUMMARY

The Medicaid statute requires states to make disproportionate share hospital (DSH) payments to hospitals treating large numbers of low-income patients. This provision is intended to recognize the disadvantaged financial situation of those hospitals because low-income patients are more likely to be uninsured or Medicaid enrollees. Hospitals often do not receive payment for services rendered to uninsured patients, and Medicaid provider payment rates are generally lower than the rates paid by Medicare and private insurance.

As with most Medicaid expenditures, the federal government reimburses states for a portion of their Medicaid DSH expenditures based on each state's federal medical assistance percentage (FMAP). While most federal Medicaid funding is provided on an open-ended basis, federal Medicaid DSH funding is capped. Each state receives an annual DSH allotment, which is the maximum amount of federal matching funds that each state is permitted to claim for Medicaid DSH payments. In FY2012, federal DSH allotments totaled $11.4 billion.

* This is an edited, reformatted and augmented version of a Congressional Research Service publication, CRS Report for Congress R42865, dated January 28, 2014.

The health insurance coverage provisions of the Patient Protection and Affordable Care Act (ACA, P.L. 111-148 as amended) are expected to reduce the number of uninsured individuals in the United States, which means there should be less need for Medicaid DSH payments. As a result, the ACA included a provision directing the Secretary of the Department of Health and Human Services to make aggregate reductions in federal Medicaid DSH allotments for each year from FY2014 to FY2020. Since the ACA, three laws have amended the DSH reductions. The Supreme Court's decision regarding the ACA Medicaid expansion does not impact these DSH reduction amounts, but states' decisions about implementing the ACA Medicaid expansion could impact the allocation of the DSH reductions across states starting in FY2016.

While there are some federal requirements that states must follow in defining DSH hospitals and calculating DSH payments, for the most part, states are provided significant flexibility. One way the federal government restricts states' Medicaid DSH payments is that the federal statute limits the amount of DSH payments for Institutions for Mental Disease and other mental health facilities.

Since Medicaid DSH allotments were implemented in FY1993, total Medicaid DSH expenditures (i.e., including federal and state expenditures) have remained relatively stable. Over this same period of time, total Medicaid DSH expenditures as a percentage of total Medicaid medical assistance expenditures (i.e., including both federal and state expenditures but excluding expenditures for administrative activities) dropped from 13% to 4%.

This report provides an overview of Medicaid DSH. It includes a description of the rules delineating how state DSH allotments are calculated and the exceptions to the rules, how DSH hospitals are defined, and how DSH payments are calculated. The DSH allotment section includes information about how the ACA DSH reductions may be allocated among the states, and the possible implications of the Supreme Court's decision regarding the ACA Medicaid expansion. The DSH expenditures section shows the trends in DSH spending and explains variation in states' DSH expenditures. Finally, the basic requirements for state DSH reports and independently certified audits are also outlined.

INTRODUCTION

Medicaid is a federal-state program providing medical assistance for low-income individuals.[1] Historically, Medicaid eligibility has generally been limited to low-income children, pregnant women, parents of dependent children, the elderly, and individuals with disabilities; however, recent changes will soon add coverage for individuals under the age of 65 with income up to 133% of the federal poverty level (FPL).[2]

Participation in Medicaid is voluntary for states, though all states, the District of Columbia, and territories[3] choose to participate. In order to participate in Medicaid, the federal government requires states to cover certain mandatory populations and benefits, but the federal government also allows states to cover optional populations and services.[4] Due to this flexibility, there is substantial variation among the states in terms of factors such as Medicaid eligibility, covered benefits, and provider payment rates.

Medicaid is jointly financed by the federal government and the states. States incur Medicaid costs by making payments to service providers (e.g., for doctor visits) and performing administrative activities (e.g., making eligibility determinations), and the federal government reimburses states for a share of these costs.[5] The federal government's share of a state's expenditures for most Medicaid services is called the federal medical assistance percentage (FMAP).[6] The FMAP varies by state and is inversely related to each state's per capita income. For FY2014, FMAP rates range from 50% (15 states) to 73% (Mississippi), and, on average, the federal contribution covers about 57% of the total cost of Medicaid in a typical year.

The Medicaid statute requires that states make disproportionate share hospital (DSH) payments to hospitals treating large numbers of low-income patients.[7] This provision is intended to recognize the disadvantaged financial situation of such hospitals because low-income patients are more likely to be uninsured or Medicaid enrollees. Hospitals often do not receive payment for services rendered to uninsured patients, and Medicaid provider payment rates are generally lower than the rates paid by Medicare and private insurance.

While most federal Medicaid funding is provided on an open-ended basis, federal Medicaid DSH funding is capped. Each state receives an annual federal DSH allotment, which is the maximum amount of federal matching funds that each state can claim for Medicaid DSH payments. In FY2012, the federal DSH allotments to states totaled $11.4 billion.

This report provides an overview of Medicaid DSH, including how state DSH allotments are calculated and the exceptions to the DSH allotments calculation; how DSH hospitals are defined and how DSH payments to hospitals are calculated; trends in DSH spending; variation in states' DSH expenditures; and requirements outlining the basic requirements for state DSH reports and independently certified audits. The DSH allotment section includes information about how the ACA DSH reductions will be allocated among the states, and the potential implications of the Supreme Court's decision in *National Federation of Independent Business v. Sebelius*.

BACKGROUND: MEDICAID DSH

Medicaid DSH payments were established in the Omnibus Budget Reconciliation Act of 1981 (OBRA 1981, P.L. 97-35) when the methodology for Medicaid payment rates to hospitals was amended.[8] Prior to OBRA 1981, state Medicaid programs were required to reimburse hospitals on a reasonable cost basis (as defined under Medicare) unless the state had approval to use an alternate payment method.[9] This law deleted the reasonable cost methodology and transferred the responsibility for determining Medicaid payment rates to the states.

A new provision required Medicaid hospital payment rates to take into account the situation of hospitals that serve a disproportionate number of "low income patients with special needs."[10] This requirement established the Medicaid DSH payments.

The inclusion of this Medicaid DSH provision in OBRA 1981 recognized that hospitals serving a disproportionate share of low income patients are particularly dependent on Medicaid payments because low income patients are mostly Medicaid enrollees and uninsured individuals.[11] Hospitals often do not receive payment for services rendered to uninsured patients, and Medicaid provider payment rates are generally lower than the rates paid by Medicare and private insurance.

States Slow to Implement DSH Programs

While the requirement to make DSH payments was originally established in 1981, many states did not make DSH payments throughout the 1980s. As a result, other federal laws were enacted with provisions aimed at getting states to make DSH payments. For instance, a provision in the Omnibus Budget Reconciliation Act of 1986 (P.L. 99-509) was aimed at supporting state flexibility to make DSH payments. Also, the Omnibus Budget Reconciliation Act of 1987 (P.L. 100-203) required states to submit a Medicaid state plan amendment[12] describing their DSH policies and establishing certain minimum qualifying standards and payments.

Sharp Increase in DSH Expenditures

DSH payments quickly became a significant portion of Medicaid spending in the early 1990s. DSH expenditures (including federal and state expenditures) grew from $1.0 billion in FY1990 to $17.4 billion in FY1992. As a percent of total Medicaid medical assistance expenditures (i.e., including federal and state spending and excluding expenditures for administrative activities), DSH expenditures grew from 1.3% of total Medicaid medical assistance expenditures in FY1990 to 15.0% in FY1992 (see **Table 1**).

The significant increase in DSH expenditures was not attributed to the laws enacted by Congress. Instead, the growth in Medicaid expenditures coincided with states' increased use of provider taxes and donations to help finance the state share of Medicaid expenditures.[13] DSH payments were a popular mechanism for returning provider taxes or donations to hospitals. Medicaid payments for regular inpatient rates were subject to federal upper payment limits, but DSH payments were uncapped and did not need to be tied to specific Medicaid enrollees or services. As a result, states could increase DSH payments by any amount, tax away the state share of the increased DSH payments through provider taxes, and thus draw down unlimited federal funds.

Limits on DSH Payments

This dramatic growth in DSH expenditures again prompted congressional action. The Medicaid Voluntary Contribution and Provider-Specific Tax Amendments of 1991 (P.L. 102-234) established ceilings on federal Medicaid DSH funding for each state.[14] Since FY1993, each state has had its own DSH limit, which is referred to as a "DSH allotment."

DSH Allotments

While most federal Medicaid funding is provided on an open-ended basis, certain types of federal Medicaid funding, such as federal DSH funding, are capped. Each state[15] receives an annual DSH allotment, which is the maximum amount of federal matching funds a state is permitted to claim for Medicaid DSH payments.[16]

The original state DSH allotments provided in FY1993 were based on each state's FY1992 DSH payments. In FY1992, some states provided relatively more DSH payments to hospitals, and, as a result, these states locked in relatively higher Medicaid DSH allotments. Other states made relatively fewer DSH payments, and these states locked in relatively lower DSH allotments.

This disparity still remains to some extent in current DSH allotments because DSH allotments are not distributed according to a formula based on the number of DSH hospitals in a state or the amount of hospital services these hospitals provide to low-income patients. However, over time, the disparity in DSH allotments was reduced by providing larger annual increases to DSH allotments for states that initially made fewer DSH payments and limiting the growth of DSH allotments for states that initially provided relatively more DSH payments.

The methodology for calculating states' annual DSH allotments has changed a number of times over the years. A history of the DSH allotment calculations is provided in **Appendix A**.

Currently, states' Medicaid DSH allotments are based on each state's prior year DSH allotment. Specifically, a state's DSH allotment is the higher of (1) a state's FY2004 DSH allotment[17] or (2) the prior year's DSH allotment increased by the percentage change in the consumer price index for all urban consumers (CPI-U) for the prior fiscal year. In FY2012, Louisiana was the only state that continued to receive its FY2004 DSH allotment.

Table 1. Total DSH Expenditures and Total DSH Expenditures as a Percentage of Total Medicaid Medical Assistance Expenditures

	DSH Expenditures (in billions)	Percent Increase	DSH Expenditures as a % of Medical Assistance Expenditures
FY1990	$1.0	NA	1.3%
FY1991	$4.7	370.0%	5.2%
FY1992	$17.4	270.2%	15.0%

Source: Payments estimated by the Urban Institute.

Notes: Total DSH expenditures include both federal and state spending on DSH payments. Total Medicaid medical assistance expenditures include federal and state spending and exclude Medicaid spending on administrative activities.

DSH = Disproportionate Share Hospital.

Each state's allotment can be no more than the greater of the prior year's allotment or 12% of its total Medicaid medical assistance expenditures (i.e., including federal and state spending and excluding expenditures for administrative activities) during the fiscal year.[18] This rule is referred to as the "12% limit."[19] This means the federal share of DSH expenditures cannot be more than 12% of each state's total Medicaid medical assistance expenditures.

In addition to the state-specific 12% limit, there is a national DSH target. Federal regulations specify that aggregate DSH payments, including federal and state expenditures for all states, should not be more than 12% of the total amount of Medicaid medical assistance expenditures for all 50 states and the District of Columbia.[20] This national limit is not an absolute cap but a target.[21] The national DSH payment limit is different from the 12% limit on state DSH allotments because the 12% national payment limit restricts both federal and state spending while the 12% limit for allotments caps only federal spending.

Due to the state-specific 12% limit for state DSH allotments, the Centers for Medicare & Medicaid Services (CMS) must publish preliminary DSH allotments before the start of the fiscal year based on estimated Medicaid expenditures. Then, after the fiscal year has ended, CMS uses actual expenditure data to calculate final DSH allotments.

CMS calculates annual allotments and publishes them in the *Federal Register.* The most recent *Federal Register* notice[22] included final DSH allotments for FY2012 and preliminary DSH allotments for FY2013. The federal DSH allotments for FY2011 through FY2013 are shown in **Table 2**.

Exceptions for Certain States

While most states' DSH allotments are determined as described above, the DSH allotments for some states are determined by an alternative method. In the past, low DSH states received higher annual percentage increases to their DSH allotments, but currently low DSH states receive the same annual percentage increases to DSH allotments as other states. Also, Hawaii and Tennessee have special statutory arrangements for the determination of their respective DSH allotments.

Low DSH States

Special rules for low DSH states were initially established by the Medicare, Medicaid, and SCHIP Benefits Improvement and Protection Act of 2000 (BIPA, incorporated into the Consolidated Appropriations Act of 2001, P.L. 106-554).[23] Subsequently, the Medicare Prescription Drug, Improvement, and Modernization Act of 2003 (MMA, P.L. 108-173) amended the definition of low DSH state, and this definition continues to apply today.

Table 2. DSH Allotments for FY2011, FY2012, and FY2013 ($ in millions)

State	FY2011 Final DSH Allotment	FY2012 Final DSH Allotment	FY2013 Preliminary DSH Allotment
Alabama	$307.5	$315.5	$323.1
Alaska[a]	20.4	20.9	21.4
Arizona	101.3	103.9	106.4
Arkansas[a]	43.1	44.3	45.3
California	1,096.3	1,124.8	1,151.8
Colorado	92.5	94.9	97.2
Connecticut	200.0	205.2	210.1
Delaware[a]	9.1	9.3	9.5
District of Columbia	61.3	62.8	64.4
Florida	200.0	205.2	210.1
Georgia	268.8	275.8	282.4
Hawaii[b]	10.0	10.0	10.2
Idaho[a]	16.4	16.9	17.3
Illinois	215.0	220.6	225.9
Indiana	213.8	219.3	224.6
Iowa[a]	39.4	40.4	41.4
Kansas	41.3	42.3	43.3
Kentucky	145.0	148.8	152.4
Louisiana	732.0	732.0	732.0
Maine	105.0	107.7	110.3
Maryland	76.3	78.2	80.1
Massachusetts	305.0	313.0	320.5
Michigan	265.0	271.9	278.4
Minnesota[a]	74.7	76.6	78.5
Mississippi	152.5	156.5	160.2
Missouri	473.8	486.1	497.8
Montana[a]	11.4	11.6	11.9
Nebraska[a]	28.3	29.0	29.7
Nevada	46.3	47.5	48.6

State	FY2011 Final DSH Allotment	FY2012 Final DSH Allotment	FY2013 Preliminary DSH Allotment
New Hampshire	160.1	164.3	168.2
New Jersey	643.8	660.5	676.4
New Mexico[a]	20.4	20.9	21.4
New York	1,606.4	1,648.1	1,687.7
North Carolina	295.0	302.7	310.0
North Dakota[a]	9.6	9.8	10.0
Ohio	406.3	416.8	426.9
Oklahoma[a]	36.2	37.2	38.0
Oregon	45.3	46.4	47.6
Pennsylvania	561.3	575.9	589.7
Rhode Island	65.0	66.7	68.3
South Carolina	327.5	336.0	344.1
South Dakota[a]	11.0	11.3	11.6
Tennessee[c]	305.5	123.6	53.1
Texas	956.3	981.2	1,004.7
Utah[a]	19.6	20.1	20.6
Vermont	22.5	23.1	23.6
Virginia	87.6	89.9	92.1
Washington	185.0	189.8	194.4
West Virginia	67.5	69.3	70.9
Wisconsin[a]	94.5	97.0	99.3
Wyoming[a]	0.2	0.2	0.2
Total	**$11,278.0**	**$11,362.1**	**$11,543.8**

Source: Department of Health and Human Services, "Medicaid Program: Disproportionate Share Hospital Allotments and Institutions for Mental Diseases Disproportionate Share Hospital Limits for FYs 2010, 2011, and Preliminary FY2012 Disproportionate Share Hospital Allotments and Limits," 77 *Federal Register* 43301, July 24, 2012; Department of Health and Human Services, "Medicaid Program: Disproportionate Share Hospital Allotments and Institutions for Mental Diseases Disproportionate Share Hospital Limits for FY2012, and Preliminary FY2013 Disproportionate Share Hospital Allotments and Limits," 78 *Federal Register* 45217, July 26, 2013.

Notes: DSH allotments are different from DSH payments. Allotments reflect the maximum amount of federal DSH funding available to states, and DSH payments are the amounts paid to hospitals.

a. These states are low DSH states. In the past, low DSH states received higher annual percentage increases to their DSH allotments than the non-low DSH states.

Currently, low DSH and other states receive the same annual percentage increases to their DSH allotments.

b. Hawaii has a special statutory arrangement that specifies the DSH allotment for the state. Beginning in FY2013, Hawaii's DSH allotment is determined the same way the DSH allotments are determined for low DSH states.

c. Tennessee has a special statutory arrangement that specifies the DSH allotment for the state. The statute limits Tennessee's Medicaid DSH payments to $91.6 million in FY2011, $70.1 million in FY2012, and $53.1 million in FY2013.

Under the MMA definition, a low DSH state is defined as a state with FY2000 DSH expenditures greater than 0% but less that 3% of its total Medicaid medical assistance expenditures (i.e., including federal and state expenditures and excluding expenditures for administrative activities) for FY2000. States determined to be low DSH states in FY2004 continue to be low DSH states regardless of their DSH expenditures in years after FY2000.

States designated as low DSH states were provided greater annual increases to their DSH allotments in order to remove some of the inequities from the initial FY1993 state DSH allotments, which were based on states' DSH expenditures in FY1992. However, increasing DSH allotments does not necessarily mean states will increase their DSH payments. The increased DSH allotments provide states with access to additional federal DSH funding if the states choose to use it.

Sixteen states qualified as low DSH states under the MMA definition, and they continue to be defined as low DSH states. These states are Alaska, Arkansas, Delaware, Idaho, Iowa, Minnesota, Montana, Nebraska, New Mexico, North Dakota, Oklahoma, Oregon, South Dakota, Utah, Wisconsin, and Wyoming.

Each year, from FY2004 through FY2008, low DSH states received a 16% increase to their DSH allotments to increase their DSH allotments relative to other states.[24]

For FY2009 and subsequent years, low DSH states receive DSH allotments equal to the prior year's allotment increased by the percent change in CPI-U for the previous fiscal year, which is the same adjustment that non-low DSH states receive.

Hawaii and Tennessee

Tennessee and Hawaii operate their state Medicaid programs under Section 1115 research and demonstration waivers,[25] which allow the Secretary of Health and Human Services (HHS) to waive various provisions of Medicaid law. Both states received waivers from making Medicaid DSH payments (among other things), and these states did not receive DSH allotments from FY1998 to FY2006. However, since FY2007, these two states received DSH allotments by special statutory authority provided through multiple laws.[26] **Table 3** shows the federal DSH funding available to Hawaii and Tennessee from FY2007 to FY2014.

Hawaii

Hawaii's DSH allotment was set at $10 million for each of FY2007 through FY2011. Under the Patient Protection and Affordable Care Act (ACA, P.L. 111-148 as amended), Hawaii's FY2012 DSH allotment was also set at $10.0 million, but the allotment was split into two periods. For the first quarter of FY2012 (i.e., October 1, 2011, to December 31, 2011), Hawaii's DSH allotment was $2.5 million. Then, for the remaining three quarters of FY2012, Hawaii's DSH allotment was $7.5 million.

For FY2013 and subsequent years, Hawaii's annual DSH allotment will increase in the same manner applicable to low DSH states. Currently, all states, including low DSH states, receive DSH allotments equal to the prior year's allotment increased by the percent change in CPI-U for the previous fiscal year.

Tennessee

The federal statute specifies that Tennessee's DSH allotment for each year from FY2007 to FY2011 is the greater of $280.0 million or the federal share of the DSH payments reflected in TennCare[27] for the demonstration year ending in 2006. In accordance with this provision, Tennessee's DSH allotment was $305.4 million (i.e., the federal share of the DSH payments reflected in TennCare for the demonstration year ending in 2006) from FY2007 to FY2011. The statute further limits the amount of federal funds available to Tennessee for DSH payments to 30% of Tennessee's DSH allotment. Under this limit, the federal DSH funding available to Tennessee for each year from FY2007 to FY2011 was $91.6 million (i.e., 30% of $305.4 million).

For the first quarter of FY2012 (i.e., October 1, 2011, through December 31, 2011), Tennessee's DSH allotment was $76.4 million[28] and subject to the 30% limit. For the last three fiscal quarters of FY2012, Tennessee received a DSH allotment of $47.2 million that was *not* subject to the 30% limit. In total, Tennessee had access to $70.1 million[29] in federal DSH funding in FY2012.

In FY2013, Tennessee had a DSH allotment of $53.1 million that is *not* subject to the 30% limit. After FY2013, the statute does not provide a federal DSH allotment to Tennessee.

Table 3. Federal DSH Funding Available to Tennessee and Hawaii FY2007 t oFY2014

Fiscal Year	Hawaii	Tennessee
FY2007	$10,000,000	$91,635,578
FY2008	$10,000,000	$91,635,578
FY2009	$10,000,000	$91,635,578
FY2010	$10,000,000	$91,635,578
FY2011	$10,000,000	$91,635,578
FY2012	$10,000,000	$70,108,895
FY2013	$10,240,000[a]	$53,100,000
FY2014	=FY2013 Allotment * (% Change in CPI-U for FY2013)	$0

Sources: Section 1923(f)(6) of the Social Security Act; Centers for Medicare & Medicaid Services, "Medicaid Program; Final FY2009 and Preliminary FY2011 Disproportionate Share Hospital Allotments, and Final FY2009 and Preliminary FY2011 Institutions for Mental Diseases Disproportionate Share Hospital Limits," 76 *Federal Register* 148, January 3, 2011; Centers for Medicare & Medicaid Services, "Medicaid Program; Disproportionate Share Hospital Allotments and Institutions for Mental Diseases Disproportionate Share Hospital Limits for FYs 2010, 2011, and Preliminary FY2012 Disproportionate Share Hospital Allotments and Limits," 77 *Federal Register* 43301, July 24, 2012; Department of Health and Human Services, "Medicaid Program: Disproportionate Share Hospital Allotments and Institutions for Mental Diseases Disproportionate Share Hospital Limits for FY2012, and Preliminary FY2013 Disproportionate Share Hospital Allotments and Limits," 78 *Federal Register* 45217, July 26, 2013.

Notes: This chart does not provide DSH allotments for Hawaii and Tennessee but the federal DSH funding available to Hawaii and Tennessee. For Hawaii, the DSH allotment and the federal DSH funding available is the same. However, Tennessee's allotment for FY2007 to FY2011 is $305,451,928, but the federal DSH funding available to Tennessee is limited to 30% of the DSH allotment ($305,451,928 * 0.30 = $91,635,578). Tennessee's DSH funding for FY2012 is the combination of $22,908,895 (30% of $76,362,982) for the first fiscal quarter and $47,200,000 for the last three fiscal quarters.

CPI-U = Consumer Price Index for all Urban consumers.

a. This is the preliminary allotment for Hawaii.

DSH Allotment Reductions

The ACA is expected to reduce the number of uninsured individuals in the United States starting in 2014 through the health insurance coverage provisions (including the ACA Medicaid expansion as impacted by the Supreme Court's ruling). Built on the premise that with fewer uninsured individuals there should be less need for Medicaid DSH payments, the ACA included a provision directing the Secretary of the Department of Health and Human Services (HHS) to make aggregate reductions in Medicaid DSH allotments equal to $500 million in FY2014, $600 million in FY2015, $600 million in FY2016, $1.8 billion in FY2017, $5.0 billion in FY2018, $5.6 billion in FY2019, and $4.0 billion in FY2020.[30 31]

Despite the assumption that reducing the uninsured would reduce the need for Medicaid DSH payments, the ACA was written so that, after the specific reductions for FY2014 through FY2020, DSH allotments would have returned to the amounts states would have received without the enactment of ACA. In other words, in FY2021, states' DSH allotments would have rebounded to their pre-ACA reduced level with the annual inflation adjustments for FY2014 to FY2021.

Since the ACA, three laws have amended the Medicaid DSH reductions. The Middle Class Tax Relief and Job Creation Act of 2012 (P.L. 112-96), the American Taxpayer Relief Act of 2012 (ATRA, P.L. 112-240), and the Continuing Appropriations Resolution, 2014 (P.L. 113-67), extended the FY2020 DSH reduction for an additional three years. Specifically, for FY2021, FY2022, and FY2023 states' DSH allotments will be the previous year DSH allotment increased by the percentage change in CPI-U for FY2020.[32] Under current law, in FY2024, states' DSH allotments will rebound to their pre-ACA reduced levels with the annual inflation adjustments for FY2014 to FY2024.

In addition, the Continuing Appropriations Resolution, 2014, eliminated the Medicaid DSH reductions for FY2014 and FY2015 and increased the FY2016 Medicaid DSH reduction to $1.2 billion.

Figure 1 shows the estimate of aggregate DSH allotments for FY2012 through FY2024 prior to ACA, under ACA, and under current law (i.e., under ACA, the Middle Class Tax Relief and Job Creation Act of 2012, ATRA, and the Continuing Appropriations Resolution, 2014). Under current law, the aggregate reductions will phase up to an estimated 43% reduction in FY2019, and in FY2023, the aggregate DSH reductions will phase down to roughly a 28% reduction. In FY2024, DSH allotments will rebound to the pre-ACA reduced levels.

Statutory Requirements for Reductions to State DSH Allotments

While the aggregate DSH reduction amounts are specified in statute, the Secretary of HHS is responsible for determining how to distribute the aggregate DSH reductions among the states using some broad statutory guidelines. The Secretary of HHS is required to impose *larger* percentage DSH reductions on states that

- have the lowest percentage of uninsured individuals (determined by the Census Bureau's data, audited hospital cost reports, and other information likely to yield accurate data) during the most recent fiscal year with available data (see **Table B-1** for states' percentage of uninsured) or

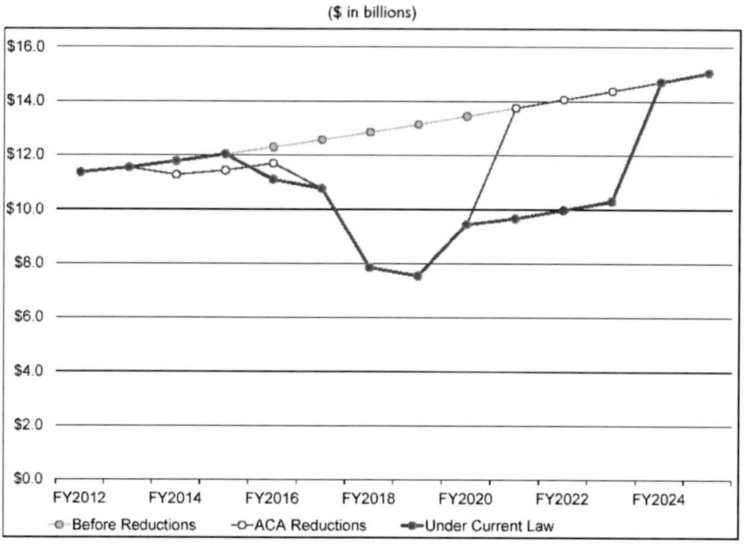

Source: CRS calculation based on final FY2012 and preliminary FY2013 DSH allotments.

Notes: The CPI-U factor used to inflate the DSH allotments is based on the factors built into the Congressional Budget Office's "The Budget and Economic Outlook: Fiscal Years 2013 to 2023" from February 2013.

DSH allotments are different from DSH expenditures. Allotments reflect the maximum amount of federal DSH funding available to states, and DSH expenditures are the amounts paid to hospitals.

Figure 1. Total DSH Allotments Before the Reductions, with the ACA Reductions, and Under Current Law.

- do *not* target their DSH payments to hospitals with high volumes of Medicaid patients and high levels of uncompensated care (excluding bad debt).

The statute also requires the Secretary of HHS to impose *smaller* percentage reductions on low DSH states (i.e., states with total Medicaid DSH payments for FY2000 between 0% and 3% of total Medicaid medical assistance expenditures). In **Appendix B**, **Table B-1** includes the low DSH state designations.

The last specification provided in statute requires the Secretary of HHS to take into account the extent to which the DSH allotment for a state was included in the budget neutrality calculation for a coverage expansion approved under a Section 1115 waiver as of July 31, 2009.

Although the statute provides the Secretary of HHS with flexibility regarding how to allocate the DSH reductions among the states, in general, states with the lowest percentage of uninsured individuals can be expected to receive relatively larger percentage DSH reductions. In addition, states that do not target their DSH payments to hospitals with the most Medicaid patients and highest uncompensated care can be expected to receive relatively larger percentage DSH reductions. Also, low DSH states should receive relatively smaller percentage DSH reductions. As a result, a non-low DSH state with a low percent of uninsured individuals that does not target its DSH payments can be expected to receive a relatively larger percentage reduction, and a low DSH state with a high percent of uninsured individuals that targets its DSH payments should receive a relatively smaller percentage DSH reduction.

The magnitude of the Medicaid DSH reductions (especially in the later years) is such that most (if not all) states are expected to have DSH allotment reductions. However, states might be able to take action to lessen the magnitude of the Medicaid DSH reductions for their state. States might be able to impact the criteria related to how they target their DSH payments and the percent of uninsured individuals. However, states do not have the ability to impact the last two criteria concerning low-DSH states and Section 1115 waiver budget neutrality calculations.

On September 18, 2013, prior to the Continuing Appropriations Resolution, 2014 eliminating the FY2014 and FY2015 reductions, CMS released a final rule regarding the methodology for allocating the DSH reductions for FY2014 and FY2015.[33] In that rule, CMS stated that a separate rule will be issued for the distribution of DSH allotment reductions for FY2016 through FY2020 because CMS does not have enough information regarding the impacts of states' decisions about implementing the ACA Medicaid expansion.

DSH Reductions and the ACA Medicaid Expansion

When CMS proposes the methodology for allocating the DSH for FY2016 and subsequent years, the allocation of the reductions may take into account states' decisions regarding the ACA Medicaid expansion.

ACA Medicaid Expansion and the Supreme Court

Beginning in 2014 (or sooner at state option), the ACA expands Medicaid to include a new mandatory eligibility group: all adults under age 65 with income up to 133% of FPL (effectively 138% FPL with the modified adjusted gross income[34] 5% FPL income disregard).[35] Originally, it was assumed that all states would implement the ACA Medicaid expansion in 2014 as required by statute because implementing the ACA Medicaid expansion was required in order for states to receive *any* federal Medicaid funding. However, on June 28, 2012, the United States Supreme Court issued its decision in *National Federation of Independent Business (NFIB) v. Sebelius*[36] finding that the federal government cannot terminate the federal Medicaid funding a state receives for its current Medicaid program if a state refuses to implement the ACA Medicaid expansion. If a state accepts the new ACA Medicaid expansion funds, it must abide by the new expansion coverage rules. However, based on the Court's opinion, it appears that a state can refuse to participate in the ACA Medicaid expansion without losing any of its current federal Medicaid matching funds.[37]

The Supreme Court decision only impacts the ACA Medicaid expansion, so the provision reducing Medicaid DSH allotments remains unchanged. This means the Supreme Court ruling does not affect the ACA Medicaid DSH reduction amounts or the statutory criteria the Secretary must use to determine a methodology for distributing the DSH reductions among states. However, the fact that some states may not implement the ACA Medicaid expansion could impact how the DSH reductions are distributed among the states. Specifically, states' decisions whether or not to implement the ACA Medicaid expansion could impact the percentage of uninsured individuals in their state, which is one of the criteria the Secretary must use to determine how to distribute the Medicaid DSH reductions among states.

ACA Expected to Reduce the Percent of Uninsured in All States

The percentage of uninsured individuals in all states is expected to decrease through a combination of ACA health insurance coverage provisions that increase access to health insurance (most of which will be effective starting in 2014). The ACA increases access to health insurance by establishing the health insurance exchanges, which are structured marketplaces for the sale and purchase of health insurance. Also, certain individuals will be eligible for federal premium tax credits and cost-sharing subsidies to help them afford health insurance.[38] The other major health insurance coverage provision included in the ACA is the Medicaid expansion.

After the Supreme Court decision, the health insurance exchanges and the premium cost-sharing subsidies are still expected to reduce the percent of uninsured individuals in all states. However, the ACA Medicaid expansion is expected to reduce the number of uninsured individuals by less than previously estimated because some states are expected to decide *not* to implement the ACA Medicaid expansion.

Even if a state does not implement the ACA Medicaid expansion, some of the individuals that would have been covered by the Medicaid expansion may still gain health insurance coverage as a part of the ACA health insurance coverage provisions. The ACA provides premium tax credits and cost-sharing subsidies to individuals with household income between 100% and 400% of FPL who do not have access to minimum essential coverage.[39] As a result, most uninsured individuals with incomes between 100% and 133% (effectively 138%) of FPL living in states that decide *not* to implement the ACA Medicaid expansion may become eligible for these premium tax credits and cost-sharing subsidies to purchase health insurance through the health insurance exchanges.[40]

Regardless of whether a state decides to implement the ACA Medicaid expansion or not, all states could experience an increase in Medicaid enrollment, due to the "woodwork" effect. This is the name for uninsured individuals who are currently eligible but not enrolled in Medicaid enrolling in Medicaid due to increased media attention and outreach efforts. The impact of the woodwork effect depends on the percentage of a state's population that is currently eligible and not enrolled in Medicaid. Estimates find that nationally 7.3 million to 9.0 million uninsured children and adults are currently eligible but not enrolled in Medicaid.[41]

How States' Decisions about the ACA Medicaid Expansion Could Impact Their DSH Reductions

Each state's percentage of uninsured individuals will be impacted by the state's decision about the ACA Medicaid expansion. However, states' percentages of uninsured individuals will be impacted by factors other than the ACA Medicaid expansion. For instance, states' percentages of uninsured individuals will also be affected by the activity in the health insurance exchanges and changes in employer-sponsored insurance coverage.

States' decisions about whether or not to implement the ACA Medicaid expansion will impact states' percentages of uninsured individuals, which could impact states' Medicaid DSH reductions. However, the magnitude of states' Medicaid DSH reductions depends on a number of factors. As mentioned previously, the statute provides the Secretary of HHS with four criteria to use in determining the allocation of the Medicaid DSH reductions, and states' percentage of uninsured individuals is just one of those criteria. The extent to which the change in each state's percent of uninsured individuals impacts each state's Medicaid DSH reductions depends on the methodology the Secretary of HHS uses to distribute the DSH reductions among states.

How states' decisions regarding the ACA Medicaid expansion impact the allocation of the DSH reductions among states depends on which states decide *not* to implement the expansion and which states decide to implement the expansion. Specifically, state characteristics that could impact the allocation of Medicaid DSH reductions are states' current percentages of uninsured individuals and states' current Medicaid eligibility levels.

If a state that currently has one of the lowest percentages of uninsured individuals chooses *not* to implement the ACA Medicaid expansion, then the percent of uninsured individuals for that state might decrease by less than for another state that does implement the expansion. Since the measure of percent of uninsured individuals is a relative ranking of states, the state's decision *not* to implement the ACA Medicaid expansion could cause the state's percent of uninsured to go from one of the lowest percentages to an average percentage. States with the lowest percentage of uninsured individuals are supposed to get the largest percentage DSH reductions, which means this state could reduce the magnitude of its DSH allotment reduction by *not* implementing the ACA Medicaid expansion.

Under the Medicaid program, some eligibility groups are mandatory, meaning that all states must cover them; other eligibility groups are optional. As a result of state differences in optional coverage, Medicaid eligibility varies significantly from state to state. If a state with relatively lower levels of

Medicaid eligibility chooses to implement the ACA Medicaid expansion, then that state would be expected to lower its percentage of uninsured individuals more than other states implementing the ACA Medicaid expansion. As a result, this state could increase the magnitude of its DSH allotment reduction by implementing the ACA Medicaid expansion.

Since the Supreme Court ruling, some states have stated their intention to implement the ACA Medicaid expansion, other states have asserted that they will not implement the expansion, and some states remain uncommitted. As of October 24, 2013, 26 states have indicated their intention to implement the ACA Medicaid expansion starting January 1, 2014.[42] However, it should be noted that states are not locked into their intentions regarding the implementation of the ACA Medicaid expansion. CMS has stated that states face no deadline for deciding when and if they will implement the ACA Medicaid expansion. Also, according to CMS, states can choose to implement the expansion and later drop Medicaid eligibility back to their pre-ACA Medicaid expansion levels.[43]

In general, states indicating they will *not* implement the ACA Medicaid expansion (e.g., Georgia, Louisiana, Mississippi, South Carolina, and Texas)[44] currently have relatively high percentages of uninsured individuals and relatively lower Medicaid eligibility levels for nondisabled adults under age 65.[45] Depending on how the Secretary chooses to distribute the Medicaid DSH reductions, by not implementing the ACA Medicaid expansion, these states might be able to reduce the magnitude of their DSH reductions.

While there are some exceptions, most of the states indicating they will implement the ACA Medicaid expansion (e.g., California, Connecticut, Delaware, Hawaii, Illinois, Maryland, Massachusetts, Minnesota, Rhode Island, Vermont, and Washington)[46] tend to have relatively lower percentages of uninsured individuals and relatively higher Medicaid eligibility levels for nondisabled adults under age 65.[47] Depending on how the Secretary chooses to distribute the Medicaid DSH reductions, by implementing the ACA Medicaid expansion, these states might increase the magnitude of their DSH reductions.

Again, depending on how the Secretary decides to distribute the DSH reductions among the states, as states' percentages of uninsured individuals decline more than other states', their percentages of the DSH reductions could increase; and as states' percentages of uninsured individuals reduce less than other states', their percentages of DSH reductions could decrease. The percentages of uninsured individuals for states that do implement the expansion are expected to reduce significantly more than those for states that do not implement the expansion. As a result, depending on how the Secretary administers the DSH reductions, states that choose *not* to implement the ACA Medicaid expansion could have relatively smaller percentage DSH reductions than they otherwise would have had because these states are expected to have relatively larger uninsured populations.

While states' decisions about the ACA Medicaid expansion have potential implications for states' Medicaid DSH reductions, states' decisions about whether or not to implement the ACA Medicaid expansion are complicated. The factors states are considering include the state cost of Medicaid coverage for the newly eligible adults; the state cost of the increase in Medicaid coverage for individuals who are currently eligible but not enrolled in Medicaid; potential state savings from current state-funded programs for individuals that will gain Medicaid coverage; and the economic value of additional health care spending for the state economy.[48]

Potential Medicaid DSH reductions are not a significant factor in states' decisions whether or not to implement the ACA Medicaid expansion because the impact of the Medicaid DSH reductions pales in comparison to other potential impacts. For instance, while the aggregate Medicaid DSH reductions from FY2016 to FY2023 total $30 billion, if all states implement the ACA Medicaid expansion it is estimated that all the ACA health insurance coverage provisions would reduce uncompensated care by $183 billion.[49]

Impact on Hospitals

Hospitals in states that are not expanding are concerned because the DSH allotments will be reduced by the same total national amount whether or not states implement the expansion. If a state implements the expansion, the uncompensated care for hospitals should decline along with the DSH allotments (though not proportionally). However, if a state chooses *not* to implement the expansion, the demand for uncompensated hospital care is expected to persist but the amount of Medicaid DSH payments hospitals receive to subsidize such care may be reduced.[50] As a result, hospitals have been encouraging their states to implement the ACA Medicaid expansion in order to reduce the uncompensated care for hospitals. Even though Medicaid provider rates are generally lower than the rates paid by private insurance or Medicare, hospitals would rather receive payment from a Medicaid patient than have no payment from an uninsured patient.

DSH PAYMENTS

Medicaid state plans must include explanations for how DSH hospitals are defined and how DSH payments are calculated. There are federal requirements that states must follow in making these determinations, but for the most part, states are provided significant flexibility in defining DSH hospitals and calculating DSH payments.

Defining DSH Hospitals

The federal government provides states with the following three criteria for identifying DSH hospitals.

- At a minimum, states must provide DSH payments to all hospitals with (1) a Medicaid inpatient utilization rate[51] in excess of one standard deviation[52] above the mean rate for the state or (2) a low-income utilization rate[53] of 25%.
- All DSH hospitals must retain at least two obstetricians with staff privileges willing to serve Medicaid patients.[54]
- A hospital *cannot* be identified as a DSH hospital if its Medicaid utilization rate is below 1%.

As long as states include all hospitals meeting the criteria, states can identify as many or as few hospitals as DSH hospitals. Because of the flexibility, there is a great deal of variation across the states in the proportion and types of hospitals designated as DSH hospitals. Some states target their DSH funds to a few hospitals, while other states provide DSH payments to all the hospitals in the state with Medicaid utilization rates above 1%.[55] For instance, in FY2007, Oregon provided DSH payments to 9 out of 58 hospitals, and New Jersey provided DSH payments to all of the hospitals in the state.[56]

Calculating DSH Payments

States are also provided a good deal of flexibility in terms of the formulas and methods they use to distribute DSH funds among DSH hospitals. The federal government provides minimum and maximum payment criteria, but otherwise federal law does not address the specific payment amounts states should provide to each DSH hospital.

States must make minimum payments to DSH hospitals using one of three methodologies:[57]

- the Medicare DSH methodology,
- a formula providing Medicaid DSH payments that increase in proportion to the percentage by which the hospital's Medicaid inpatient utilization rate exceeds one standard deviation above the mean, or
- a formula that varies DSH payments according to the type of hospitals.[58]

DSH payments to individual hospitals are subject to a cap.[59] This hospital-specific limit prohibits DSH payments from being greater than 100% of the cost of providing inpatient and outpatient services to Medicaid and uninsured patients less payments received from Medicaid and uninsured patients.[60]

The Definition of Uninsured

Under the hospital-specific DSH limit, uninsured is defined in the statute as individuals who "have no health insurance (or other source of third-party coverage) for the services furnished during the year."[61] In the past, CMS has provided conflicting guidance regarding this definition, in January 2012, CMS issued a proposed rule to address this issue.[62]

The hospital-specific limit was implemented through the Omnibus Reconciliation Act of 1993 (P.L. 103-66), and, following the passage of the law, CMS did not issue a rule. However, CMS did issue a State Medicaid Director Letter delineating the agency's interpretation of the statute, which stated that individuals who have no health insurance (or other third party coverage) for the services provided during the year include those "who do not possess health insurance which applies to the service for which the individual sought treatment."[63]

This interpretation remained in effect until January 19, 2009, which was the effective date for the 2008 DSH final rule implementing the DSH auditing and reporting requirements (these requirements are discussed later in the report in the section titled "State Reporting and Auditing Requirements").[64] In promulgating the 2008 DSH final rule, CMS defined "uninsured" as individuals who do not have a legally liable third party payer for hospital services.[65] The 2008 DSH final rule relied on the existing regulatory definition of creditable coverage developed to implement the Health Insurance Portability and Accountability Act of 1996 (P.L. 104-191). The definition of uninsured from the 2008 final rule superseded the guidance from the 1994 State Medicaid Director Letter.

Concerns were raised about the new definition of uninsured because this definition appeared to exclude from uncompensated care (for Medicaid DSH purposes) the costs of many services that were provided to individuals with creditable coverage but were outside the scope of such coverage. For instance, the definition excluded individuals who exhausted their insurance benefits and who reached lifetime insurance limits for certain services, as well as services not covered in a benefit package.

In response to these concerns, CMS issued a proposed rule on January 18, 2012, that would change the definition of uninsured for Medicaid DSH purposes to a service-specific definition. The proposed definition would require a determination of whether, for each specific service furnished during the year, the individual has third party coverage. As a result, the proposed definition would include services not within a covered benefit package and services beyond the annual and lifetime limits.[66]

Institutions for Mental Disease (IMD) DSH Limits

Federal statute limits the amount of DSH payments for IMDs[67] and other mental health facilities.[68] DSH payments to IMDs and other mental health facilities above the state-specific dollar limit are not eligible for federal matching funds.

Each state receives an IMD DSH limit that is the lesser of:

- a state's FY1995 total IMD and other mental health facility DSH expenditures (i.e., including both state and federal spending) applicable to the state's FY1995 DSH allotment as reported on the Form CMS-64 as of January 1, 1997, or
- the amount equal to the product of the state's current year total DSH allotment and the applicable percentage, which is the lesser of 33% or the percent of FY1995 DSH expenditures that went to mental health facilities.

The IMD DSH limits fit within the state DSH allotments. In other words, when DSH payments to hospitals and IMDs and other mental health facilities are summed together, the total is required to be less than or equal to the state's DSH allotments in **Table 2**.

As with the DSH allotments, the IMD DSH limits are published in periodic *Federal Register* notices. In **Appendix C**, **Table C-1** includes each state's preliminary IMD DSH limit for FY2012.

($ in billions)

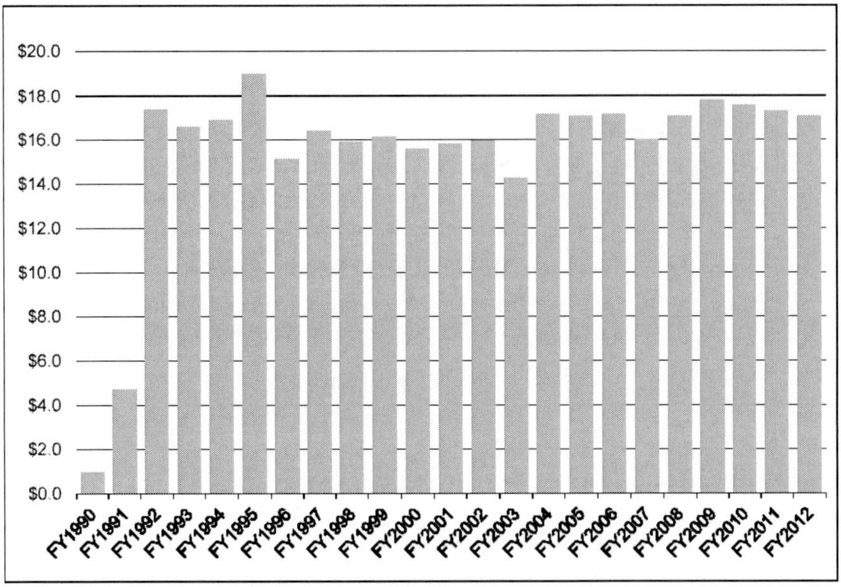

Source: Payments estimated by the Urban Institute for FY1990-FY1992; data from CMS for FY1993-FY1996; CMS-64 data for FY1997-FY2012.

Notes: Total Medicaid DSH expenditures include both federal and state spending and payments to both hospitals and institutions for mental disease. Data for FY2012 is preliminary.

DSH expenditures are different from DSH allotments. DSH expenditures are the amounts paid to hospitals, and DSH allotments reflect the maximum amount of federal DSH funding available to states.

Figure 2.Total Medicaid DSH Expenditures, FY1990-FY2012.

DSH Expenditures

The implementation of the DSH allotments effectively controlled the significant growth of DSH expenditures from the early 1990s. As shown in

Figure 2, total Medicaid DSH expenditures (i.e., including both federal and state expenditures) have remained relatively stable since the implementation of the federal DSH allotments in FY1993. In FY2012, DSH expenditures totaled $17.1 billion, and the federal share of those payments was $9.6 billion.[69]

While Medicaid DSH expenditures have been relatively stable, total Medicaid medical assistance expenditures (i.e., including federal and state expenditures and excluding expenditures on administrative activities) have generally grown at a rate faster than the economy as measured by the gross domestic product for the period of FY1990 to FY2009. Since FY2010, total Medicaid DSH expenditures have decreased slightly from year to year.

The law establishing DSH allotments (i.e., Medicaid Voluntary Contribution and Provider-Specific Tax Amendments of 1991, P.L. 102-234) specified a national DSH payment limit equal to 12% of the total amount of Medicaid medical assistance spending (i.e., including federal and state expenditures and excluding expenditures for administrative activities) for all 50 states and the District of Columbia.[70] This is a target but not an absolute cap.

As mentioned earlier, the national DSH payment limit is different from the state-specific 12% limit on state DSH allotments because the 12% national payment limit restricts both federal and state spending while the 12% limit for allotments caps only federal spending. The national DSH payment target states that aggregate DSH payments (including federal and state expenditures) should not be more than 12% of the total amount of Medicaid medical assistance expenditures for all 50 states and the District of Columbia. The federal statute limits state DSH allotments (i.e., the maximum amount of Medicaid DSH federal funds) to no more than 12% of each state's total Medicaid medical assistance expenditures (i.e., including federal and state expenditures but excluding administrative expenditures), which means the federal share of DSH expenditures cannot be more than 12% of each state's total Medicaid medical assistance expenditures.

This means if a state receives a federal DSH allotment equal to 12% of its total Medicaid medical assistance expenditures and the state uses all of its federal DSH allotment, then with the state matching funds, the state would provide DSH payments in excess of 12% of its total Medicaid medical assistance expenditures. As a result, it is possible that the national DSH target could be surpassed even if state DSH allotments are subject to the 12% limit. However, as shown in **Figure 3**, the implementation of DSH allotments effectively brought DSH payments under the 12% national target within a few years. DSH allotments were implemented in FY1993, and total DSH expenditures fell below 12% of total Medicaid medical assistance expenditures in FY1996. In FY2012, total DSH expenditures were 4.2% of the total Medicaid medical assistance expenditures.

FY1990 to FY2012

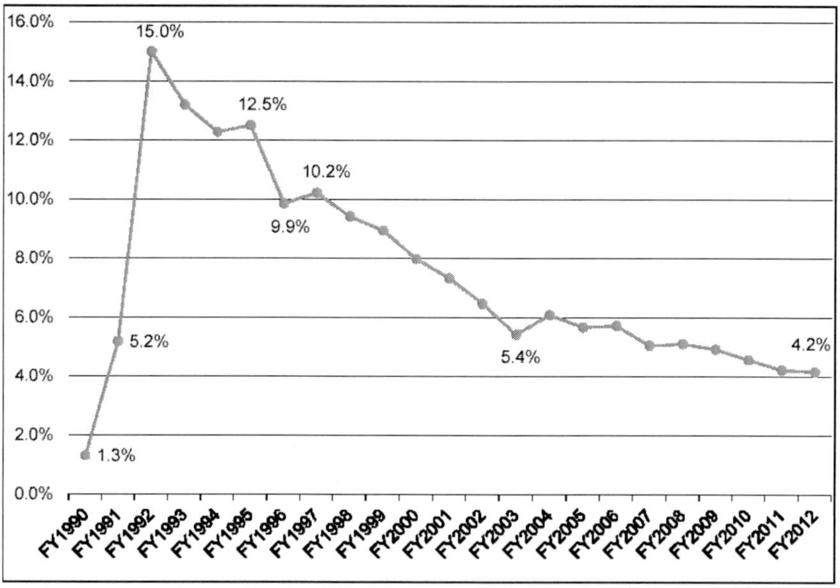

Sources: CRS calculation using DSH payment estimates from the Urban Institute for FY1990-FY1992; DSH payment data from Centers for Medicare & Medicaid Services (CMS) for FY1993-FY1996; DSH payment data for FY1997-FY2011 and medical assistance expenditure data for FY1990-FY2011 from Form CMS-64 data.

Notes: Total DSH expenditures and total Medicaid medical assistance expenditures (i.e., excluding expenditures for administrative activities) include both the federal and state expenditures. Data for FY2012 is preliminary.

Figure 3. Total DSH Expenditures as a Percentage of Total Medicaid Medical Assistance Expenditures.

DSH expenditures are highly concentrated in a few states. As shown in **Figure 4**, five states (New York, California, Texas, New Jersey, and Pennsylvania) accounted for more than half of the FY2011 DSH expenditures, and 10 states accounted for over two-thirds of all DSH expenditures. It makes sense that some of these states (New York, California, Texas, New Jersey, Pennsylvania, and Ohio) accounted for a large portion of the total Medicaid

DSH expenditures because these states were among the top 10 highest-spending states in terms of total medical assistance expenditures (i.e., including federal and state expenditures and excluding expenditures for administrative activities) for FY2011. On the other hand, Missouri, Louisiana, South Carolina, and Alabama ranked 15th, 22nd, 25th, and 26th (respectively) in terms of total medical assistance expenditures (i.e., including federal and state expenditures and excluding expenditures for administrative activities) for FY2011, but these states were among the top 10 highest spending states in terms of Medicaid DSH expenditures. This means Missouri, Louisiana, South Carolina, and Alabama spend larger proportions of their Medicaid budgets on Medicaid DSH payments relative to most other states.[71]

FY2011

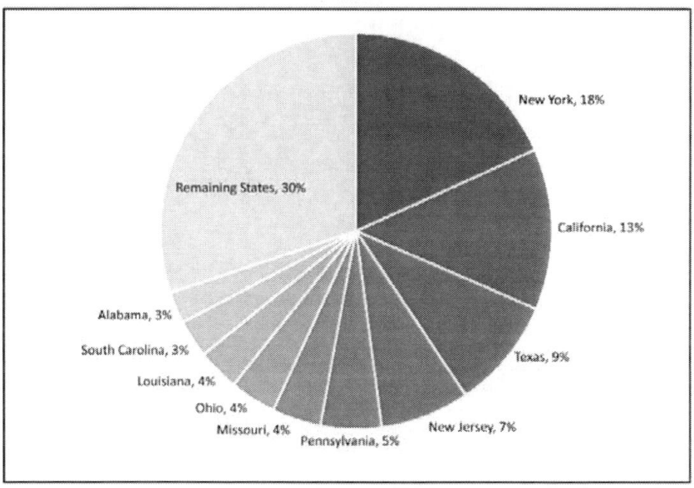

Source: CRS calculation using Centers for Medicare & Medicaid Services' Form CMS-64 data from FY2011.

Notes: The states included in the "remaining states" category had DSH expenditures that accounted for less than 3% of total DSH expenditures. In **Appendix D, Table D-1** shows state-by-state DSH spending. FY2011 is the most recent data available.

Figure 4. States' Share of Total Medicaid DSH Expenditures.

FY2011

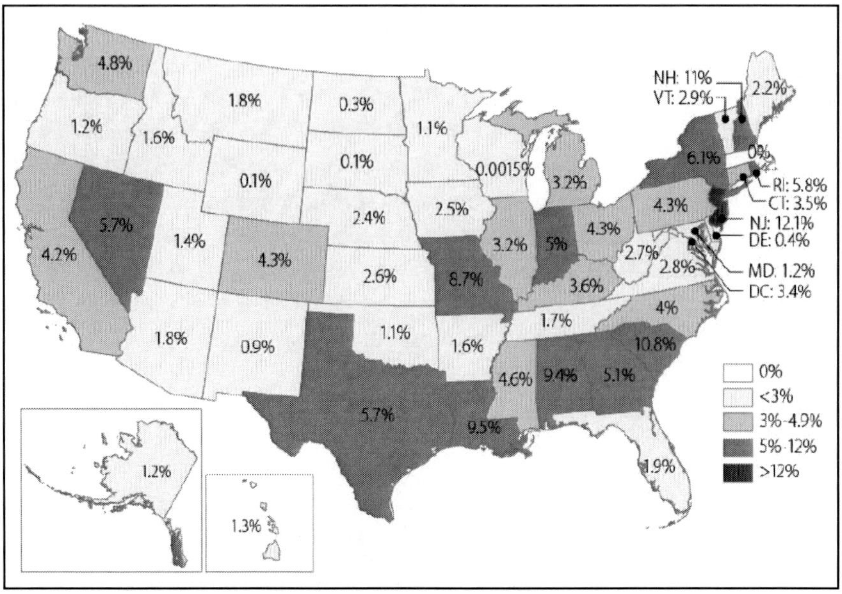

Source: CRS calculation using Centers for Medicare & Medicaid Services' Form CMS-64 data for FY2011,

Notes: Total DSH expenditures and total Medicaid medical assistance expenditures (i.e., excluding expenditures for administrative activities) include both the federal and state share of expenditures. FY2011 is the most recent data available.

Massachusetts does not have DSH expenditures because Massachusetts' Section 1115 waiver allows the state to use its DSH allotment to fund the state's Health Safety Net which reduces the number of uninsured in Massachusetts. In **Appendix D, Table D-1** shows each state's total DSH expenditures and total Medicaid medical assistance expenditures.

Figure 5. Total State DSH Expenditures as a Percentage of Total Medicaid Medical Assistance Expenditures.

State Variation

As mentioned previously, there is significant variation among the states in how each state DSH program is structured, and there is also variation from state to state with respect to DSH expenditures. Two distinct differences are (1) the percent of a state's total Medicaid medical assistance expenditures (i.e., including federal and state expenditures and excluding expenditures for administrative activities) a state's DSH expenditures account for and (2) the proportion of DSH payments going to hospitals versus IMDs.

DSH As a Percentage of Total Medical Assistance Expenditures

Figure 5 shows FY2011 total DSH expenditures (i.e., including both federal and state expenditures) as a percentage of total Medicaid medical assistance expenditures (i.e., including federal and state expenditures and excluding expenditures for administrative activities). DSH expenditures made in FY2011 ranged from 0.1% of total Medicaid medical assistance expenditures in South Dakota and Wyoming to 12.1% in New Jersey.

In FY2011, one state (New Jersey) had DSH expenditures in excess of 12% of total Medicaid medical assistance expenditures,[72] which was the threshold used to determine "high" DSH states when DSH allotments were first implemented.[73] This is down from FY1993, when 21 states were considered "high" DSH states.

Hospital versus IMD

Nationally, 83% of DSH expenditures are allocated to hospitals, and the remaining 17% is distributed to IMDs and other mental health facilities. This distribution varies by state. As shown in **Figure 6**, in FY2011, most states targeted their DSH expenditures to hospitals, with 15 states[74] allocating all of their DSH expenditures to hospitals. Other states focused their DSH expenditures on IMDs and other mental health facilities. Three states (South Dakota, Maine, and Delaware) made all of their DSH expenditures to IMDs and other mental health facilities.

STATE REPORTING AND AUDITING REQUIREMENTS

Since FY1993, each state has been required to provide quarterly reports with information about the aggregate DSH payments made to hospitals. Then, in 1997 and again in 2003, Congress enhanced the DSH reporting requirements in response to HHS Office of the Inspector General audits and Government Accountability Office reports detailing state violations in the DSH program.

The Balanced Budget Act of 1997 (BBA, P.L. 105-33) required states to provide an annual report to the Secretary of HHS describing the method used to target DSH funds and to calculate DSH payments. Then, in 2003, MMA mandated that beginning in state plan rate year[75] (SPRY) 2005, states were required to submit annual reports and independently certified audits.[76]

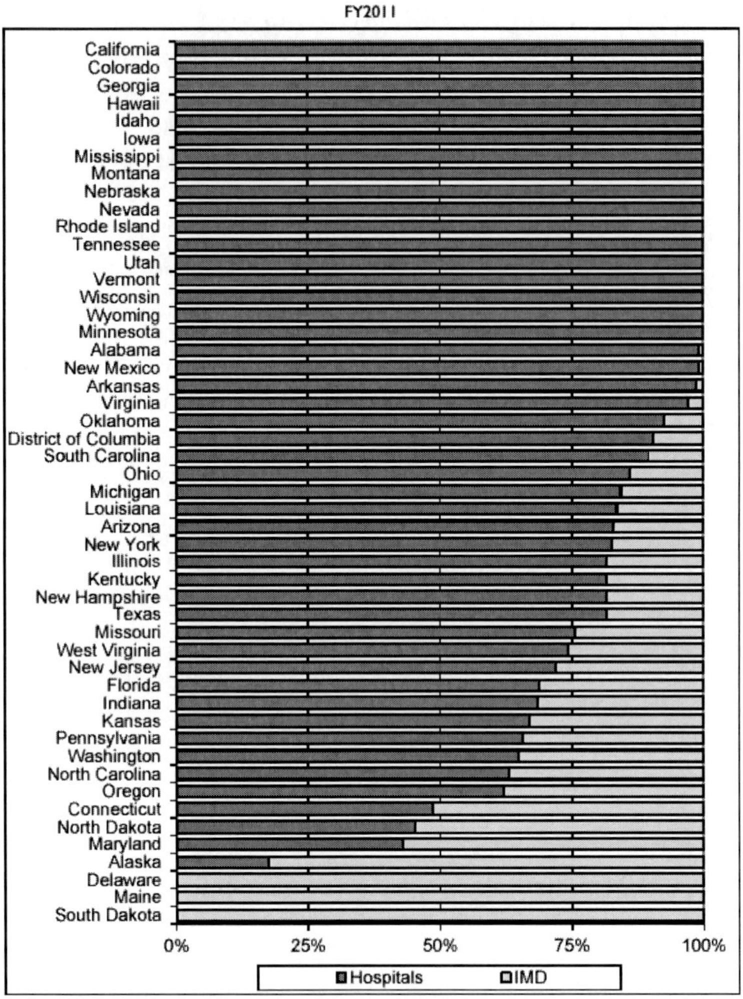

Source: CRS calculation using Centers for Medicare & Medicaid Services' Form CMS-64 data from FY2011.

Notes: **Table D-1** shows each state's hospital and IMD DSH expenditures. FY2011 is the most recent data available.

IMD = Institutions for Mental Diseases and other mental health facilities.

Figure 6. Proportion of State DSH Expenditures Allocated to Hospitals and IMDs.

States' annual DSH reports must provide detailed information about each hospital receiving a DSH payment. For each hospital, the report must include the following information: the hospital-specific DSH limit, the Medicaid inpatient utilization rate, the low income utilization rate, state-defined DSH qualification criteria, Medicaid basic payments, other supplemental payments, total Medicaid uncompensated care, total uninsured uncompensated care, federal Section 1011 payments,[77] and DSH payments.

The annual independent certified audits must verify that hospitals retain the DSH payment; DSH payments are made in accordance with the hospital-specific DSH limits; uncompensated care only includes inpatient and outpatient services; and the state separately documented and retains records of DSH payments (including the methodology for calculating each hospital's DSH payments).

The annual independent certified audits must be completed by the last day of the federal fiscal year ending three years from the end of the SPRY under audit. The annual DSH reports are due at the same time as the independent certified audits. If a state does not submit the independent certified audit by this deadline, the state could lose the federal DSH matching funds for the SPRYs subsequent to the date the audit is due.[78]

To ensure a period for developing and refining the reporting and auditing techniques, findings of state reports and audits for SPRY2005 to SPRY2010 will not be given weight except to the extent that the findings draw into question the reasonableness of the state uncompensated care cost estimates used for calculations of prospective DSH payments. For SPRY2011 and after, audit findings demonstrating that DSH payments exceed the hospital-specific cost limit will be regarded as discovery of overpayment to providers. This will require the state to return the federal share of the overpayment to the federal government (unless the DSH payments are redistributed to other qualifying hospitals).[79]

CONCLUSION

Since DSH allotments were implemented in FY1993, DSH payments have remained relatively stable. Over the same period of time, Medicaid medical assistance expenditures (i.e., including federal and state expenditures and excluding expenditures for administrative activities) have generally grown at a rate faster than the economy (as measured by the gross domestic product). As a result, total DSH expenditures have dropped as a percentage of total

Medicaid medical assistance expenditures from 15.0% in FY1992 to 4.2% in FY2011.

Over the next few years, DSH expenditures will continue to decline as a percentage of Medicaid medical assistance expenditures due to the ACA DSH reductions. The impact of these reductions will vary by state according to the uninsurance rate of each state; whether a state is a "low DSH state"; and how a state targets its DSH payments.

Currently, the DSH reductions are slated to end in FY2023 with state DSH allotments returning to the level states would have received without the DSH reduction for FY2024 and subsequent years. However, the future of Medicaid DSH payments is uncertain because Congress may decide to extend the DSH reductions again. Also, as states build experience with the ACA Medicaid expansion, the role of DSH in Medicaid may be revisited and modified by Congress.

APPENDIX A. A CHRONOLOGY OF STATE DSH ALLOTMENTS CALCULATIONS

The Medicaid Voluntary Contribution and Provider-Specific Tax Amendments of 1991 (P.L. 102-234) established ceilings on federal Medicaid DSH funding for each state. Since FY1993, each state has had its own DSH limit, which is referred to as "DSH allotments." These allotments are calculated by the Centers for Medicare & Medicaid Services (CMS) and promulgated in the *Federal Register*. The methodology for calculating these allotments has changed a number of times over the years, and these different methodologies are described below.[80]

FY1993

The original state DSH allotments provided in FY1993 were based on each state's FY1992 DSH payments. This resulted in funding inequities because states that had been providing relatively more DSH payments to hospitals in FY1992 locked in higher Medicaid DSH allotments (and vice versa). As a result, the DSH allotment a state receives is not entirely based on the number of DSH hospitals in the state or the hospital services provided in DSH hospitals to low-income patients.

FY1994 to FY1997

The DSH allotments for FY1994 to FY1997 were based on each state's prior year DSH allotment. The annual growth for each state's DSH allotment depended on whether a state was classified as a "high-DSH" or "low-DSH" state. States with DSH expenditures greater than 12% of their total Medicaid medical assistance expenditures (i.e., federal and state Medicaid expenditures excluding expenditures for administrative activities) were classified as "high-DSH" states, and "high-DSH" states did not receive an increase to their DSH allotment. States with DSH expenditures less than 12% of their total Medicaid medical assistance expenditures were classified as "low-DSH" states, and the growth factor for the DSH allotment for "low-DSH" states was the projected percentage increase for each state's total Medicaid expenditures (i.e., including federal and state spending) for the current year. However, "low-DSH" states' DSH allotments could not exceed 12% of each state's total medical assistance expenditures.[81]

FY1998 to FY2000

Provisions included in the Balanced Budget Act of 1997 (BBA, P.L. 105-33) reduced Medicaid DSH expenditures by replacing the state DSH allotment calculations with *fixed* state DSH allotments specified in statute for FY1998 through FY2002.[82] The aggregate fixed allotments for FY1998 totaled $10.3 billion, which was a 50% decrease from the aggregate FY1997 DSH allotments. The aggregate allotments for FY1999 and FY2000 decreased to $10.0 billion and $9.3 billion respectively.

Adjustments for Specific States

A number of legislative adjustments were made to the BBA fixed DSH allotments. The Departments of Labor, Health and Human Services, and Education, and Related Agencies Appropriations Act, 1998 (P.L. 105-78) increased the FY1998 DSH allotments for Minnesota and Wyoming. The Omnibus Consolidated and Emergency Supplemental Appropriations Act, 1999 (P.L. 105-277) increased the FY1999 DSH allotments for Minnesota, New Mexico, and Wyoming. The Medicare, Medicaid, and SCHIP Balanced Budget Refinement Act of 1999 (included in the Consolidated Appropriations Act 2000, P.L. 106-113) increased the FY2000, FY2001, and FY2002 DSH allotments for the District of Columbia, Minnesota, New Mexico, and Wyoming.

FY2001 and FY2002

The fixed state allotments were supposed to last through FY2002 with the aggregate DSH allotments slated to decrease in FY2001 and again in FY2002. However, the Medicare, Medicaid, and SCHIP Benefits Improvement and Protection Act of 2000 (BIPA, which was incorporated into the Consolidated Appropriations Act of 2001, P.L. 106-554) eliminated the DSH reductions for FY2001 and FY2002 and provided states with increases to their DSH allotments. Specifically, the DSH allotments for those two years were determined by increasing each state's prior year DSH allotment by the percent change in the Consumer Price Index for all Urban Consumers (CPI-U) for the prior fiscal year. These state DSH allotments could not exceed 12% of a state's total medical assistance expenditures for the allotment year. This is referred to as the 12% rule.[83]

Extremely Low DSH States

BIPA also established a special rule for DSH allotments for "extremely low DSH states," which were defined as states with FY1999 DSH expenditures greater than 0% and less than 1% of total Medicaid medical assistance expenditures (i.e., federal and state Medicaid expenditures excluding expenditures for administrative activities).[84] The FY2001 DSH allotments for extremely low DSH states were increased to 1% of each state's FY2001 total medical assistance expenditures. Then, the FY2002 DSH allotments for extremely low DSH states were each state's FY2001 DSH allotment increased by the percentage change in CPI-U for FY2001, subject to the 12% rule.[85]

FY2003

For non-extremely low DSH states, FY2003 DSH allotments were each state's FY2002 fixed DSH allotment determined in BBA (i.e., not states' actual DSH allotment for FY2002 as provided by BIPA) increased by the percent change in CPI-U for FY2002, subject to the 12% rule. For most states, the FY2002 state DSH allotments provided by BBA were less than the actual state allotments states received in FY2002. As a result, in general, FY2003 DSH allotments were lower than the allotments states received in FY2002.[86] This was not the case for extremely low DSH states, which received FY2003 DSH allotments based on their actual FY2002 DSH allotment increased by percentage change in CPI-U for FY2002.[87]

FY2004

The Medicare Prescription Drug, Improvement, and Modernization Act of 2003 (MMA, P.L. 108-173) addressed the drop in DSH allotments for many states from FY2002 to FY2003 by exempting FY2002 DSH allotment amounts from the 12% rule and providing a 16% increase in DSH allotments for FY2004.

Low DSH States

MMA also discontinued the special arrangement for extremely low DSH states and instead established low DSH states—defined as those states in which total DSH payments for FY2000 were less than 3% of the state's total Medicaid medical assistance expenditures. For such states, FY2004 DSH allotments were each state's FY2003 DSH allotment increased by 16%.

After FY2004

State DSH allotments for years after FY2004 are set to be equal to each state's FY2004 DSH allotment, unless a state's allotment as determined by the calculation in place prior to MMA would equal or exceed the FY2004 allotment for that state. For any years a state's DSH allotments would be higher under the pre-MMA calculation, that state's DSH allotment will be equal to its DSH allotment from the prior fiscal year increased by the percentage change in the CPI-U for the prior fiscal year, subject to the 12% rule.[88]

Low DSH States

By statute, the definition of low DSH state is a state with FY2000 DSH expenditures greater than 0% but less that 3% of total Medicaid medical assistance expenditures for FY2000. So states determined to be low DSH states in FY2004 continue to be low DSH states regardless of the states' DSH expenditures in years after FY2000.

For FY2004 through FY2008, low DSH states received DSH allotments in each year equal to each state's prior year DSH allotment increased by 16%, subject to the 12% rule. For FY2009 forward, the allotment for low DSH states is equal to the prior year allotment amount increased by the percentage change in the CPI-U (subject to the 12% rule), which is the same DSH increase provided to non-low DSH states.

District of Columbia

The Deficit Reduction Act of 2005 (DRA, P.L. 109-171) increased the fixed DSH allotments for the District of Columbia for FY2000, FY2001, and FY2002 from $32 million to $49 million. This change was effective as of October 1, 2005. Increasing the District of Columbia's DSH allotments for FY2000 to FY2002 was done for the purposes of determining the District of Columbia's FY2006 DSH allotment. This change made the District of Columbia's DSH allotment for FY2006 $57.7 million, which was a $20.0 million increase over what the District of Columbia would have gotten without the change. The provision took effect on October 1, 2005, and applies to FY2006 and subsequent fiscal years.

FY2009 and FY2010

The American Recovery and Reinvestment Act of 2009 (ARRA, P.L. 111-5) temporarily increased states' DSH allotments for FY2009 and FY2010.[89] Specifically, ARRA provided states with a FY2009 DSH allotment that was 102.5% of the FY2009 allotment states would have received without ARRA. Then, states'FY2010 DSH allotments were 102.5% of each state's FY2009 DSH allotment as determined under ARRA. For both years, the ARRA DSH provisions were not applied to the DSH allotments for states that would have had a higher DSH allotment as determined without application of the ARRADSH provisions. After FY2010, states' annual DSH allotments returned to being determined as they were prior to the enactment of ARRA.[90]

APPENDIX B. ACA DSH REDUCTIONS

Under the Patient Protection and Affordable Care Act (ACA, P.L. 111-148 as amended), it is expected that the ACA health insurance coverage expansions will reduce the number of uninsured individuals served by hospitals starting in 2014. For this reason, theoretically, there will be less need for DSH payments. As a result, the ACA directed the Secretary of the Department of Health and Human Services (HHS) to make aggregate reductions in Medicaid DSH allotments from FY2014 through FY2020.[91]

To achieve these aggregate reductions, the Secretary will be required to impose the *largest* percentage reductions on states that

- have the lowest percentage of uninsured individuals (determined on the basis of data from the Bureau of the Census, audited hospital cost reports, and other information likely to yield accurate data) during the most recent fiscal year with available data or
- do not target their DSH payments to hospitals with high volumes of Medicaid patients, and hospitals that have high levels of uncompensated care (excluding bad debt).

ACA also requires the Secretary of HHS to impose *smaller* percentage reduction on low DSH states as defined in Section 1923(f)(5)(B) of the Social Security Act. Low DSH states are those states where total Medicaid DSH payments (including federal and state share) for FY2000 were between 0% and 3% of total Medicaid medical assistance expenditures (i.e., including Medicaid spending on health care and excluding expenditures for administrative activities).

Table B-1 shows each state's percentage of uninsured ranked from highest to lowest. The table also indicates low DSH state designations. The information in the table is the most recent data available.

In general, states with the lowest percentage of uninsured individuals can be expected to receive larger percentage DSH reductions. Also, low DSH states can be expected to receive smaller percentage DSH reductions. Also, as states' percentages of uninsured individuals increase or decrease relative to other states', due to implementing or not implementing the ACA Medicaid expansion among other reasons, states' percentages of the DSH reductions could increase or decrease accordingly starting in FY2016.

Regardless of whether a state decides to implement the ACA Medicaid expansion or not, all states could experience a reduction in the percentage of uninsured individuals, due to the woodwork effect. This is the name for uninsured individuals that are currently eligible but not enrolled in Medicaid coming out of the woodwork to enroll in Medicaid due to increased media attention and outreach efforts. The impact of the woodwork effect depends on the percentage of a state's population that is currently eligible and not enrolled in Medicaid. Estimates find that, nationally, 7.3 million to 9.0 million uninsured children and adults are currently eligible but not enrolled in Medicaid.[92]

Similarly, the uninsured population for all states is expected to decline as new individuals purchase private health insurance, as the health insurance exchanges and federal premium tax credits and cost-sharing subsidies become available in 2014.[93]

Table B-1. State Factors for DSH Reductions—Percentage of Uninsured Individuals and Low DSH State Designation

State	Percent Uninsured, 2012	Rank for Percent Uninsured	Low DSH State
Texas	22.5%	1	
Nevada	22.2%	2	
Alaska	20.5%	3	X
Florida	20.1%	4	
Georgia	18.4%	5	
New Mexico	18.4%	6	X
Oklahoma	18.4%	7	X
Montana	18.0%	8	X
California	17.9%	9	
Arizona	17.6%	10	
Mississippi	17.0%	11	
Louisiana	16.9%	12	
South Carolina	16.8%	13	
North Carolina	16.6%	14	
Arkansas	16.4%	15	X
Idaho	16.2%	16	X
Wyoming	15.4%	17	X
Oregon	14.9%	18	X
Colorado	14.7%	19	
Utah	14.5%	20	X
West Virginia	14.4%	21	
Indiana	14.3%	22	
Kentucky	13.9%	23	

State	Percent Uninsured, 2012	Rank for Percent Uninsured	Low DSH State
Tennessee	13.9%	24	
Washington	13.9%	25	
Missouri	13.6%	26	
Alabama	13.3%	27	
Illinois	12.8%	28	
New Jersey	12.7%	29	
Kansas	12.6%	30	
Virginia	12.5%	31	
Ohio	11.5%	32	
South Dakota	11.5%	33	X
Michigan	11.4%	34	
Nebraska	11.3%	35	X
Rhode Island	11.1%	36	
New York	10.9%	37	
New Hampshire	10.6%	38	
Maryland	10.3%	39	
Maine	10.2%	40	
North Dakota	10.0%	41	X
Pennsylvania	9.8%	42	
Connecticut	9.1%	43	
Wisconsin	9.0%	44	X
Delaware	8.8%	45	X
Iowa	8.4%	46	X
Minnesota	8.0%	47	X
Hawaii	6.9%	48	
Vermont	6.5%	49	
District of Columbia	5.9%	50	
Massachusetts	3.9%	51	

Source: U.S. Census Bureau, American Community Survey, 2012 1-year estimates; Department of Health and Human Services, "Medicaid Program: Disproportionate Share Hospital Allotments and Institutions for Mental Diseases Disproportionate Share Hospital Limits for FY2012, and Preliminary FY2013 Disproportionate Share Hospital Allotments and Limits," 78 *Federal Register* 45217, July 26, 2013.

Note: DSH = Disproportionate Share Hospital.

APPENDIX C. IMD DSH LIMITS

Under Sections 1923(h) of the Social Security Act, states cannot collect Medicaid federal matching funds for DSH payments to IMDs and other mental health facilities that are in excess of state-specific aggregate limits. The aggregate limit for each state is the lesser of a state's FY1995 DSH expenditures to IMDs and other mental health facilities or the amount equal to the product of a state's current year DSH allotment and the applicable percentage (i.e., the percentage of FY1995 DSH expenditures paid to IMDs and other mental health facilities with a maximum of 33%). **Table C-1** shows states' final IMD DSH limits for FY2012 and preliminary limits for FY2013.

Table C-1. States' IMD DSH Limits FY2012 and FY2013

State	FY2012 Final Limits	FY2013 Preliminary Limits
Alabama	$3,054,805	$3,050,798
Alaska	$6,897,334	$7,062,870
Arizona	$19,163,608	$18,702,314
Arkansas	$579,363	$574,939
California	$777,960	$777,960
Colorado	$297,388	$297,388
Connecticut	$52,786,863	$52,786,863
Delaware	$3,056,482	$3,139,053
District of Columbia	$4,581,595	$4,581,595
Florida	$67,721,531	$69,346,847
Georgia	$0	$0
Hawaii	$0	$0
Idaho	$0	$0
Illinois	$44,704,138	$44,704,138
Indiana	$72,377,386	$74,114,444
Iowa	$0	$0
Kansas	$13,967,566	$14,302,787
Kentucky	$26,651,979	$26,416,088
Louisiana	$80,310,122	$80,310,122
Maine	$35,553,804	$36,407,095
Maryland	$25,818,834	$26,438,486
Massachusetts	$52,817,527	$52,817,527

State	FY2012 Final Limits	FY2013 Preliminary Limits
Michigan	$89,731,028	$91,884,573
Minnesota	$2,628,607	$2,628,607
Mississippi	$0	$0
Missouri	$131,490,365	$127,179,885
Montana	$0	$0
Nebraska	$1,025,941	$1,010,002
Nevada	$0	$0
New Hampshire	$47,376,974	$47,376,974
New Jersey	$178,685,231	$178,685,231
New Mexico	$176,720	$175,981
New York	$302,500,000	$302,500,000
North Carolina	$99,889,258	$102,286,600
North Dakota	$547,617	$516,677
Ohio	$59,937,114	$59,404,548
Oklahoma	$2,090,951	$2,094,879
Oregon	$12,566,330	$12,472,447
Pennsylvania	$190,043,546	$194,604,591
Rhode Island	$1,249,751	$1,229,129
South Carolina	$50,626,422	$50,763,367
South Dakota	$444,243	$422,155
Tennessee	$0	$0
Texas	$170,301,413	$173,460,560
Utah	$663,463	$650,565
Vermont	$5,223,253	$5,083,555
Virginia	$3,885,134	$3,885,134
Washington	$62,642,416	$64,145,834
West Virginia	$13,715,772	$13,606,227
Wisconsin	$2,719,014	$2,683,527
Wyoming	$0	$0
Total	**$1,941,278,848**	**$1,954,582,362**

Source: Department of Health and Human Services, "Medicaid Program: Disproportionate Share Hospital Allotments and Institutions for Mental Diseases Disproportionate Share Hospital Limits for FY2012, and Preliminary FY2013 Disproportionate Share Hospital Allotments and Limits," 78 Federal Register 45217, July 26, 2013.

Notes: DSH = Disproportionate Share Hospital. IMD = Institutions for Mental Diseases.

Appendix D. State-by-State DSH Expenditures

There is significant variation from state to state with respect to DSH expenditures. Two distinct differences are (1) the proportion of DSH payments going to hospitals and IMDs and (2) total DSH payments as a percent of total Medicaid medical assistance expenditures (i.e., including federal and state expenditures and excluding expenditures for administrative activities).

Nationally, 83% of Medicaid DSH expenditures are allocated to hospitals, and the remaining 17% is distributed to IMDs and other mental health facilities. This distribution varies by state. As shown in **Table D-1**, in FY2011, most states targeted their DSH expenditures to hospitals with 15 states allocating all of their DSH expenditures to hospitals. However, some states focused their DSH expenditures on IMDs and other mental health facilities. Three states (South Dakota, Maine, and Delaware) used all of their DSH expenditures for IMDs and other mental health facilities.

Table D-1 also shows FY2011 total DSH expenditures (i.e., including both federal and state expenditures) as a percentage of total Medicaid medical assistance expenditures (i.e., including federal and state expenditures and excluding expenditures for administrative activities). DSH expenditures made in FY2011 ranged from 0.1% of total Medicaid medical assistance expenditures in South Dakota and Wyoming to 12.1% in New Jersey.

Table D-1. DSH Expenditures byType and DSH Expenditures as a Percentage of Medical Assistance Expenditures FY2011 ($ in millions)

State	DSH Expenditures			Total Medical Assistance	DSH Payments as a Percentage of Medical Assistance Expenditures
	Hospital	IMD	Total		
Alabama	$445.8	$3.3	$449.1	$4,793.2	9.4%
Alaska	2.6	12.6	15.2	1,290.5	1.2%
Arizona	137.3	28.5	165.8	8,988.4	1.8%

State	DSH Expenditures			Total Medical Assistance	DSH Payments as a Percentage of Medical Assistance Expenditures
	Hospital	IMD	Total		
Arkansas	61.2	0.8	62.0	3,951.8	1.6%
California	2,274.9	0.3	2,275.3	54,305.8	4.2%
Colorado	185.0	0.0	185.0	4,349.0	4.3%
Connecticut	98.1	103.3	201.4	5,812.4	3.5%
Delaware	0.0	5.6	5.6	1,391.7	0.4%
District of Columbia	66.2	7.1	73.3	2,129.5	3.4%
Florida	241.2	108.9	350.1	18,127.9	1.9%
Georgia	410.1	0.0	410.1	8,064.6	5.1%
Hawaii	20.0	0.0	20.0	1,523.9	1.3%
Idaho	24.7	0.0	24.7	1,514.7	1.6%
Illinois	334.2	75.7	409.8	12,836.0	3.2%
Indiana	223.9	102.8	326.7	6,566.4	5.0%
Iowa	81.9	0.0	81.9	3,317.1	2.5%
Kansas	46.8	23.1	69.9	2,669.2	2.6%
Kentucky	165.4	37.4	202.8	5,652.1	3.6%
Louisiana	501.0	99.2	600.2	6,297.5	9.5%
Maine	0.0	51.5	51.5	2,356.2	2.2%
Maryland	38.0	50.4	88.4	7,319.5	1.2%
Massachusetts	0.0	0.0	0.0	13,007.4	0.0%
Michigan	326.8	61.1	387.9	12,062.9	3.2%
Minnesota	89.3	0.1	89.4	8,271.2	1.1%
Mississippi	204.1	0.0	204.1	4,410.8	4.6%
Missouri	528.2	171.4	699.6	8,011.2	8.7%
Montana	17.0	0.0	17.0	954.5	1.8%
Nebraska	38.5	0.0	38.5	1,637.3	2.4%
Nevada	88.4	0.0	88.4	1,562.9	5.7%
New Hampshire	121.1	27.5	148.6	1,348.2	11.0%
New Jersey	912.5	357.4	1,269.9	10,501.1	12.1%
New Mexico	28.9	0.3	29.1	3,317.6	0.9%
New York	2,606.7	551.5	3,158.2	51,711.7	6.1%
North Carolina	258.5	150.5	408.9	10,297.1	4.0%
North Dakota	0.8	1.0	1.8	701.9	0.3%

Table D-1. (Continued)

State	DSH Expenditures			Total Medical Assistance	DSH Payments as a Percentage of Medical Assistance Expenditures
	Hospital	IMD	Total		
Ohio	569.5	93.4	662.9	15,533.3	4.3%
Oklahoma	40.7	3.3	44.0	4,008.3	1.1%
Oregon	32.9	20.0	52.9	4,386.3	1.2%
Pennsylvania	571.4	297.9	869.3	20,395.0	4.3%
Rhode Island	122.7	0.0	122.7	2,098.7	5.8%
South Carolina	474.6	56.1	530.7	4,930.8	10.8%
South Dakota	0.0	0.5	0.5	750.2	0.1%
Tennessee	139.2	0.0	139.2	7,970.0	1.7%
Texas	1,286.6	292.5	1,579.1	27,847.4	5.7%
Utah	24.0	0.0	24.0	1,733.3	1.4%
Vermont	37.4	0.0	37.4	1,281.9	2.9%
Virginia	189.4	5.9	195.3	6,893.8	2.8%
Washington	226.7	122.1	348.9	7,335.0	4.8%
West Virginia	54.4	18.9	73.3	2,740.2	2.7%
Wisconsin	0.1	0.0	0.1	6,878.4	0.0%
Wyoming	0.8	0.0	0.8	527.2	0.1%
Total	**$14,349.6**	**$2,941.7**	**$17,291.3**	**$408,148.0**	**4.2%**

Source: CRS calculation using Centers for Medicare & Medicaid Services' Form CMS-64 Data for FY2011.

Notes: Medicaid medical assistance expenditures exclude administrative expenditures. FY2011 is the most recent data available.

DSH = Disproportionate Share Hospital. IMD = Institutions for Mental Diseases.

a Massachusetts does not have DSH expenditures because Massachusetts' Section 1115 waiver allows the state to use its DSH allotment to fund the state's Health Safety Net, which is used to offset uncompensated care hospital costs, to pay for designated state health programs, and to subsidize premiums for Commonwealth Care (a program that provides sliding-scale premium subsidies for private health plan coverage for uninsured persons at or below 300% of the federal poverty level).

End Notes

[1] For more information about the Medicaid program, see CRS Report RL33202, Medicaid: A Primer, by Elicia J. Herz.

[2] The Patient Protection and Affordable Care Act (ACA, P.L. 111-148 as amended) establishes 133% of federal poverty level (FPL) based on modified adjusted gross income (MAGI) as the new mandatory minimum Medicaid income eligibility level. The law also specifies that an income disregard in the amount of 5% FPL will be deducted from an individual's income when determining Medicaid eligibility based on MAGI. Thus, the effective upper income eligibility threshold for individuals in this new eligibility group will be 138% FPL.

[3] The territories are American Samoa, Guam, the Commonwealth of the Northern Mariana Islands, Puerto Rico, and the Virgin Islands.

[4] On June 28, 2012, the United States Supreme Court issued its decision in *National Federation of Independent Business v. Sebelius*, finding that the federal government cannot terminate current Medicaid program federal matching funds if a state refuses to implement the Medicaid expansion required by ACA. If a state accepts the new ACA Medicaid expansion funds, it must abide by the new expansion coverage rules, but, based on the Court's opinion, it appears that a state can refuse to participate in the expansion without losing any of its current federal Medicaid matching funds.

[5] For an overview of Medicaid financing issues, see CRS Report R42640, *Medicaid Financing and Expenditures*, by Alison Mitchell.

[6] For more information about the FMAP rate, see CRS Report R42941, *Medicaid's Federal Medical Assistance Percentage (FMAP), FY2014*, by Alison Mitchell and Evelyne P. Baumrucker

[7] The Medicare program also makes DSH payments. Medicaid and Medicare DSH hospital payments are similar in that the major basis for designating hospitals to receive payments is the proportion of services provided to low-income patients. However, Medicaid and Medicare have different criteria for identifying DSH hospitals, and the programs have different calculations for determining DSH payment amounts.

[8] The DSH provision was included in a package of provisions referred to as the "Boren amendment" after its sponsor, Senator David Boren from Oklahoma.

[9] The Secretary of Health and Human Services could approve an alternate system only if the Secretary determined that (1) a reasonable cost was paid (though the state could develop its own methods and standards for determining what was reasonable) and (2) the reasonable cost did not exceed the amount which would be determined reasonable under Medicare.

[10] §1902(a)(13)(A)(iv) of the Social Security Act.

[11] Conf. Rept. 97-208.

[12] A Medicaid State Plan is a contract between a state and the federal government describing how that state administers its Medicaid program, and a state is required to submit a state plan amendment when the state intends to change its Medicaid program.

[13] In the mid-1980s, states began using provider taxes along with provider donations to help finance Medicaid. Essentially, Medicaid providers would donate funds or agree to be taxed, and the revenue from these taxes and donations would be used to finance a portion of the state's share of Medicaid expenditures. Some states were borrowing funds from Medicaid providers in order to draw down federal funds and increase Medicaid payment rates to the same providers that had paid taxes or donated funds. The providers were often fully reimbursed for the cost of their tax payment or donation. For more information about Medicaid provider taxes and donations, see CRS Report RS22843, *Medicaid Provider Taxes*, by Alison Mitchell.

[14] Also, the Medicaid Voluntary Contribution and Provider-Specific Tax Amendments (P.L. 102-234) restricted the use of provider donations in financing Medicaid to extremely limited

situations and limited states' ability to draw down federal Medicaid matching funds with provider tax revenue.

[15] State is defined as the 50 states and the District of Columbia. DSH allotments are not provided for the five territories (i.e., America Samoa, Commonwealth of the Northern Mariana Islands, Guam, Puerto Rico, and the Virgin Islands). (§1923(f)(9) of the Social Security Act).

[16] Each state's regular FMAP rate is used to determine the federal share of DSH payments.

[17] The Medicare Prescription Drug, Improvement, and Modernization Act of 2003 (MMA, P.L. 108-173) addressed the drop in DSH allotments for many states from FY2002 to FY2003 by providing a 16% increase in DSH allotments for states in FY2004. If a state's FY2004 DSH allotment is higher than the DSH allotment calculated under the pre-MMA calculation, then the state has received that higher DSH allotment amount since FY2004.

[18] §1923(f)(3)(B) of the Social Security Act.

[19] When DSH allotments were first implemented, a state with DSH expenditures greater than 12% of its total Medicaid medical assistance expenditures were classified as "high-DSH" states, and "high-DSH" states did not receive annual increases to their DSH allotment.

[20] 42 C.F.R. §447.297.

[21] This means if a state receives a federal DSH allotment equal to 12% of its total Medicaid medical assistance expenditures and the state uses all of its federal DSH allotment, then with the state matching funds, the state would provide DSH payments in excess of 12% of its total Medicaid medical assistance expenditures. As a result, the national DSH target could be surpassed. However, in FY2011, DSH payments were well below the national DSH target with total DSH payments (i.e., including federal and state expenditures) amounting to 4.2% of total Medicaid medical assistance expenditures (i.e., including federal and state expenditures but excluding administrative services).

[22] Department of Health and Human Services, "Medicaid Program: Disproportionate Share Hospital Allotments and Institutions for Mental Diseases Disproportionate Share Hospital Limits for FY2012, and Preliminary FY2013 Disproportionate Share Hospital Allotments and Limits," 78 *Federal Register* 45217, July 26, 2013.

[23] BIPA defined extremely low DSH states as those for which FY1999 total DSH payments (federal and state shares) were greater than zero but less than 1% of the state's total Medicaid medical assistance expenditures (i.e., the federal and state share of Medicaid expenditures excluding administrative expenditures). (§1923(f)(5)(A) of the Social Security Act.)

[24] §1923(f)(5)(B) of the Social Security Act.

[25] §1115 of the Social Security Act gives the Secretary of Health and Human Services authority to approve experimental, pilot, or demonstration projects that promote the objectives of the Medicaid and CHIP programs.

[26] These laws include the Tax Relief and Health Care Act of 2006 (P.L. 109-432), the Medicare, Medicaid, and SCHIP Extension Act of 2007 (P.L. 110-173), the Medicare Improvements for Patients and Providers Act of 2008 (P.L. 110-275), the Children's Health Insurance Program Reauthorization Act of 2009 (P.L. 111-3), and the Patient Protection and Affordable Care Act (P.L. 111-148 as amended).

[27] TennCare is the name of Tennessee's Medicaid program, which operates under a §1115 waiver.

[28] This amount is one-fourth of $305,451,928, which was the DSH allotment for Tennessee for each year from FY2007 to FY2011.

[29] $70,108,895 = $22,908,895 (i.e., 30% of $76,362,982) + $47,200,000

[30] §1923(f)(7) of the Social Security Act.

[31] The United States Supreme Court decision in *National Federation of Independent Business (NFIB) v. Sebelius* (issued June 28, 2012) did not impact this provision of ACA. Only the provision expanding Medicaid eligibility to all nonelderly individuals was impacted by the Supreme Court decision.

[32] §1923(f)(8) of the Social Security Act.

[33] Centers for Medicare & Medicaid Services, "Medicaid Program; State Disproportionate Share Hospital Allotment Reductions," 78 *Federal Register* 57293, September 18, 2013.

[34] The modified adjusted gross income (MAGI) is an income definition used for determining Medicaid income eligibility for certain individuals beginning in 2014. For more information about MAGI, see CRS Report R41997, *Definition of Income for Certain Medicaid Provisions and Premium Credits in ACA*, coordinated by Christine Scott.

[35] Historically, Medicaid eligibility was generally limited to low-income children, pregnant women, parents of dependent children, the elderly, and people with disabilities. For more information about the ACA changes to Medicaid, see CRS Report R41210, *Medicaid and the State Children's Health Insurance Program (CHIP) Provisions in ACA: Summary and Timeline*, by Evelyne P. Baumrucker et al.

[36] 132 S. Ct. 2566 (2012).

[37] For a discussion of the Supreme Court's decision on the Medicaid expansion, *see* CRS Report R42367, *Medicaid and Federal Grant Conditions After NFIB v. Sebelius: Constitutional Issues and Analysis*, by Kenneth R. Thomas.

[38] For more information about the American Health Benefit Exchanges and the federal subsidies, see CRS Report R42663, *Health Insurance Exchanges Under the Patient Protection and Affordable Care Act (ACA)*, by Bernadette Fernandez and Annie L. Mach.

[39] The definition of minimum essential coverage is broad. It includes Medicare Part A, Medicaid, the State Children's Health Insurance Program (CHIP), Tricare, the TRICARE for Life program, the veteran's health care program, the Peace Corps program, a government plan (local, state, federal) including the Federal Employees Health Benefits Program (FEHBP) and any plan established by an Indian tribal government, any plan offered in the individual, small group or large group market, a grandfathered health plan, and any other health benefits coverage, such as a state health benefits risk pool, as recognized by the Secretary of HHS in coordination with the Treasury Secretary.

[40] Uninsured individuals with household income below 100% of FPL and living in a state that does not implement the ACA Medicaid expansion are not eligible for the premium tax credits or cost-sharing subsidies.

[41] Benevieve M. Kenney, Lisa Dubay, Stephen Zuckerman, and Michael Huntress, *Opting Out of the Medicaid Expansion under the ACA: How Many Uninsured Adults Would not Be Eligible for Medicaid?*, The Urban Institute Health Policy Center, July 5, 2012; Benjamin D. Sommers and Arnold M. Epstein, "Perspective: Why States Are So Miffed about Medicaid - Economics, Politics, and the "Woodwork Effect"," *The New England Journal of Medicine*, vol. 365, no. 2, pp. 100-102 (July 14, 2011).

[42] Centers for Medicare & Medicaid Services, *State Medicaid and CHIP Income Eligibility Standards Effective January 1, 2014*, October 24, 2013.

[43] Centers for Medicare & Medicaid Services, *Frequently Asked Questions on Exchanges, Market Reforms and Medicaid*, December 10, 2012.

[44] Centers for Medicare & Medicaid Services, *State Medicaid and CHIP Income Eligibility Standards Effective January 1, 2014*, October 24, 2013.

[45] U.S. Census Bureau, American Community Survey, 2011; Medicaid and CHP Payment and Access Commission, *Report to the Congress on Medicaid and CHIP*, March 2012.

[46] State Refor(u)m, *Tracking Medicaid Expansion Decisions: A Closer Look at Legislative Activity*, Updated May 9, 2013; The Advisory Board Company, *Where Each State Stands on ACA's Medicaid Expansion: A Roundup of What Each State's Leadership Has Said about their Medicaid Plans*, Updated May 24, 2013; Alavere, *State Reform Insights*, Updated May 30, 2013.

[47] Ibid.

[48] Deborah Bachrach, *Medicaid Expansion: Factors for State Evaluation*, Presentation at Alliance for Health Reform and Kaiser Family Foundation briefing titled *The Medicaid Expansion: What's at Stake for States?*, November 30, 2012.

[49] John Holahan, Matthew Buettgens, and Caitlin Carroll, et al., *The Cost and Coverage Implications of the ACA Medicaid Expansion: National and State-by-State Analysis*, Kaiser Commission on Medicaid and the Uninsured, Publication #8384, November 2012.

[50] Letter from the Republican Governors Public Policy Committee to President Barack Obama dated July 10, 2012, available at http://www.scribd.com/doc/99730375/Medicaid-and-Exchange-Letter-Final. Sarah Kliff, "The super wonky reason states may join the Medicaid expansion," *The Washington Post*, July 8, 2012. Bob Neal, *The Fiscal and Economic Impacts of Medicaid Expansion in Mississippi, 2014-2025*, Mississippi Public Universities University Research Center, October 2012.

[51] The formula for the Medicaid utilization rate is the number of days of care furnished to Medicaid beneficiaries during a given period divided by the total number of days of care provided during the period. (§1923(b)(2) of the Social Security Act).

[52] The "standard deviation" is a statistical measure of the dispersion of hospitals' utilization rates around the average; the use of this measure identifies hospitals whose Medicaid utilization is unusually high.

[53] The formula for the low-income utilization rate is the sum of two fractions. The first fraction is total Medicaid revenue for services plus other payments from state and local governments divided by the total amount of hospital revenue for patient services. The second fraction is the total amount of hospital charges for inpatient hospital services minus the total amount of revenue from state and local governments divided by total hospital charges. (§1923(b)(3) of the Social Security Act).

[54] There are exceptions to this rule for children's hospitals, hospitals that do not offer non-emergency obstetric services, and certain rural hospitals. (§1923(d) of the Social Security Act).

[55] Courtney Burke, "Health Reform: Uncompensated Care Costs and Reductions In Medicaid DSH Payments," *Health Affairs Blog*, October 15, 2010.

[56] CRS review of DSH annual reports and the American Hospital Association Hospital Statistics (2012 Edition).

[57] §1923(c) of the Social Security Act.

[58] If a state chooses to reimburse according to the type of hospital, the state must ensure that all hospitals of each type are treated equally and payments are reasonably related to the hospitals' Medicaid or low-income patient cost, volume, or proportion of Medicaid or low-income patients.

[59] §1923(g) of the Social Security Act.

[60] In California, the hospital-specific cap for public hospitals is 175% of the unreimbursed costs. California's hospital-specific DSH cap for public hospitals was established in the Balanced Budget Act of 1997 (P.L. 105-33) and made permanent by the Medicare, Medicaid, and SCHIP Balanced Budget Refinement Act of 1999 (which was included in the Consolidated Appropriations Act of 2000, P.L. 106-113).

[61] §1923(g)(1)(A) of the Social Security Act.

[62] A final rule has not been published. (Department of Health and Human Services' Centers for Medicare & Medicaid, "Medicaid Program; Disproportionate Share Hospital Payments - Uninsured Definition," 77 *Federal Register* 2500, January 18, 2012.)

[63] State Medicaid Directors letter, August 17, 1994.

[64] The reporting requirements originally established in the Balanced Budget Act of 1997 (P.L. 105-33) were extended by the Medicare Prescription Drug, Improvement, and Modernization Act of 2003 (MMA, P.L. 108-173).

[65] Department of Health and Human Services' Centers for Medicare & Medicaid Services, "Medicaid Program: Disproportionate Share Hospital Payments," 73 *Federal Register* 77904, December 19, 2008.

[66] Department of Health and Human Services' Centers for Medicare & Medicaid, "Medicaid Program; Disproportionate Share Hospital Payments - Uninsured Definition," 77 *Federal Register* 2500, January 18, 2012.

[67] An "institution for mental diseases" is defined as "a hospital, nursing facility, or other institution of more than 16 beds, that is primarily engaged in providing diagnosis, treatment, or care of persons with mental diseases, including medical attention, nursing care and related services." (§1905(i) of the Social Security Act)

[68] §1923(h) of the Social Security Act.

[69] In FY2012, the federal DSH allotments (i.e., the maximum amount of federal matching funds that each state can claim for Medicaid DSH payments) to states totaled $11.4 billion.

[70] 42 C.F.R. §447.297.

[71] In FY2011, only New Jersey and New Hampshire spent a larger proportion of their Medicaid budget (i.e., Medicaid DSH payments as a percentage of medical assistance expenditures) than Missouri, Louisiana, South Carolina, and Alabama.

[72] The 12% limit on DSH allotments caps the federal share of DSH expenditures to no more than 12% of a state's total Medicaid medical assistance expenditures. However, when the federal DSH allotment funds are matched with the state share of the Medicaid DSH payments, a state could provide DSH payments in excess of 12% of its total Medicaid medical assistance expenditures.

[73] When DSH allotments were first implemented, states with DSH expenditures greater than 12% of their total Medicaid medical assistance expenditures were classified as "high-DSH" states, and "high-DSH" states did not receive annual increases to their DSH allotment.

[74] The fifteen states allocating all of their DSH expenditures to hospitals are Colorado, Georgia, Hawaii, Idaho, Iowa, Mississippi, Montana, Nebraska, Nevada, Rhode Island, Tennessee, Utah, Vermont, Wisconsin, and Wyoming.

[75] Medicaid state plan rate year means the 12-month period defined by a state's approved Medicaid state plan in which the state estimates eligible uncompensated care costs and determines corresponding DSH payments as well as all other Medicaid payment rates. The period usually corresponds with the state's fiscal year or the federal fiscal year but can correspond to any 12-month period defined by the state as the Medicaid state plan rate year.

[76] §1923(j) of the Social Security Act.

[77] Under §1011 of MMA, hospitals, physicians, and ambulance service providers are eligible for §1011 payments for services furnished to the following types of patients: undocumented aliens; aliens who have been paroled into a United States port of entry for the purpose of receiving eligible services; and Mexican citizens permitted to enter the United States on a laser visa, issued in accordance with the requirements of regulations prescribed under the Immigration and Nationality Act. (Centers for Medicare & Medicaid Services, *Section 1011: Fact Sheet Federal Reimbursement of Emergency Health Services Furnished to Undocumented Alien.*)

[78] 42 CFR 455.304(a).

[79] Department of Health and Human Services, Centers for Medicare & Medicaid Services, "Medicaid Program; Disproportionate Share Hospital Payments," 73 *Federal Register* 77904, December 19, 2008.

[80] Tennessee and Hawaii have had special statutory arrangements for their federal DSH funding since FY2007.

[81] The definition of "low-DSH" state has changed over the years.

[82] §1923(f)(2) of the Social Security Act.

[83] Department of Health and Human Services' Center for Medicare & Medicaid Services, "Medicaid Program; Disproportionate Share Hospital Payments," 69 *Federal Register* 15850, March 26, 2004.

[84] Ten states were classified as extremely low DSH states for FY2001 and FY2002: Arkansas, Idaho, Iowa, Montana, Nebraska, North Dakota, South Dakota, Utah, Virginia, and Wisconsin.

[85] Department of Health and Human Services' Center for Medicare & Medicaid Services, "Medicaid Program; Disproportionate Share Hospital Payments," 69 *Federal Register* 15850, March 26, 2004.

[86] This is referred to as the "DSH dip."

[87] Department of Health and Human Services' Center for Medicare & Medicaid Services, "Medicaid Program; Disproportionate Share Hospital Payments," 69 *Federal Register* 15850, March 26, 2004.

[88] Ibid.

[89] The ARRA increase to DSH allotments did not apply to the allotments for Hawaii and Tennessee.

[90] §5001(e) of ARRA specifies that the ARRA temporary increase to the FMAP does not apply to DSH payments.

[91] The FY2020 DSH reduction was extended to FY2023 through the Middle Class Tax Relief and Job Creation Act of 2012 (P.L. 112-96), the American Taxpayer Relief Act of 2012 (P.L. 112-240), and the Continuing Appropriations Resolution, 2014 (P.L. 113-67). Also, the Continuing Appropriations Resolution, 2014 eliminated the Medicaid DSH reductions for FY2014 and FY2015 and increased the FY2016 reduction to $1.2 billion.

[92] Benevieve M. Kenney, Lisa Dubay, Stephen Zuckerman, and Michael Huntress, *Opting Out of the Medicaid Expansion under the ACA: How Many Uninsured Adults Would not Be Eligible for Medicaid?*, The Urban Institute Health Policy Center, July 5, 2012; Benjamin D. Sommers and Arnold M. Epstein, "Perspective: Why States Are So Miffed about Medicaid - Economics, Politics, and the "Woodwork Effect"," *The New England Journal of Medicine*, vol. 365, no. 2, pp. 100-102 (July 14, 2011).

[93] For more information about the American Health Benefit Exchanges and the federal subsidies, see CRS Report R42663, *Health Insurance Exchanges Under the Patient Protection and Affordable Care Act (ACA)*, by Bernadette Fernandez and Annie L. Mach.

INDEX

D

E

F

G

H

I

L

M

N

O

W

Y